John Ward

Historical sketches of the rise and progress of methodism in Bingley and the circuit

John Ward

Historical sketches of the rise and progress of methodism in Bingley and the circuit

ISBN/EAN: 9783742842282

Manufactured in Europe, USA, Canada, Australia, Japa

Cover: Foto ©Andreas Hilbeck / pixelio.de

Manufactured and distributed by brebook publishing software (www.brebook.com)

John Ward

Historical sketches of the rise and progress of methodism in Bingley and the circuit

NEW WESLEYAN SCHOOLS, BINGLEY.

HISTORICAL SKETCHES

OF THE

RISE AND PROGRESS OF METHODISM

IN

BINGLEY,

WITH

BRIEF NOTICES OF OTHER PLACES IN THE CIRCUIT.

BY JOHN WARD,
WESLEYAN MINISTER.

"ACCORDING TO THIS TIME IT SHALL BE SAID OF JACOB AND OF ISRAEL, WHAT HATH GOD WROUGHT!"—NUMBERS XXV ch. XXV v.

BINGLEY:
JOHN HARRISON AND SON, PRINTERS, YORK PLACE,
1863.

PREFACE.

When the writer entered upon his present sphere of labour, he found floating about various interesting facts and incidents connected with Methodism in this town, which were likely soon to pass into oblivion. Some of these he has caught hold of and grouped together in the form now presented to the reader. The living links connecting the days of Mr. Wesley with the present generation are becoming very few. Here and there may be found individuals who heard and saw that venerable man. In a short time they will be all gone. It is desirable in every place where he laboured that recollections of his visits should be preserved. As Bingley was favoured in this respect, and as he frequently refers in his Journal to his labours in this place, these visits, together with traditions connected with the same, have here been placed on record.

The writer, in tracing the past history of Methodism in this locality, labours under the disadvantage of not having had a personal acquaintance with many of the good men whom he has named. He has tried, however, to realise their characters, to live in their times, and, with the nearest possible approach to truth, endeavoured to represent them in the following sketches. Inaccuracies will probably be found, but it is hoped there will not be many. Cheapness also has been aimed at, in order that the Methodist working-man and woman might possess, at a small cost, a record of the rise and progress of the church of their fathers; and also that the scholars of our sabbath schools might be supplied with some information respecting the former days of Methodism in this town and neighbourhood. He has, therefore, directed his observations chiefly to Bingley, as well as left out some things which might not have been deemed uninteresting. He felt anxious to include also extended descriptions of Methodism in other places in the circuit, but fearing that by so doing the cost would be thereby much increased, he has been compelled to limit himself to a somewhat brief account of them.

He wishes to acknowledge the kindness of Mr. Hardcastle of Keighley, in supplying him with the list of members in the olden times; and also to state that Mr. H. is at present engaged in preparing a History of Methodism in Keighley, which will probably include further information respecting Methodism in this town when it was in the Keighley Circuit.

If these pages shall contribute to the edification and profit of those for whom they are principally designed, their end will be answered, and the labour of putting them together will be fully compensated.

JOHN WARD.

Chapel House, Park Road,
  Bingley, 1863.

HISTORICAL SKETCHES, &c.

THE town of Bingley is pleasantly situated on the left bank of the river Aire. The valley in which it stands is celebrated for its picturesqueness and beauty, but it is generally admitted that this part of it bears away the palm. The natives of the place are proud of its scenery, and call it the "Throstle nest of old England." Nicholson, the Airedale poet, in high and glowing strains, sung the beauties of his native vale. He says:—

> "For finer walks, for more sequestered bowers,
> For cooler grottos, and for richer flowers,
> For streams that wind more beautiful along,
> For birds with louder chorus to their song,
> For all that gen'rous nature can bestow,
> All Yorkshire scenes to Bingley vale must bow."

The town itself presents no striking features. The useful has evidently superseded the ornamental. Its architecture contrasts unfavourably with the beautiful hills around, and supplies another illustration of those well known words, "God made the country, and man made the town."

It is a place, however, of some antiquity. William the Conqueror gave the lordship of Bingley to Erneis de Berun. In the twelfth year of the reign of King John, William de Gant held a charter for a market here. The cross and market-house bear the marks of great antiquity, and evidently show that as a market town it has at one time been a place of considerable importance. In 1621 a castle stood on what is called Bailey hill. In 1668 the manor was in the possession of Robert Benson, Esq., whose son was created the first lord Bingley. At the siege of Bradford the Bingley club-men rendered effective service on the side of the parliamentarians, and the army of General Fairfax encamped in this immediate neighbourhood. The church, a plain and ancient structure, was restored in the reign of Henry VIII, and in the same reign the free grammar school was founded. The Independents have long had a cause here. Oliver Heywood, one of the ejected ministers, originated a church shortly after his separation from the church of England, which has continued ever since. The old place of worship in Chapel lane, now occupied as dwelling-houses, was erected towards the end of the seventeenth century, and Accepted Lister, a noted preacher of his day, was the minister from 1695 to 1702. The Baptist chapel was erected in 1760, and has been subsequently enlarged. The Quakers had formerly a meeting house at Crossflatts, but their Society becoming extinct in this neighbourhood, the building has been turned into cottages. The burial ground adjoining is now used as garden allotments, in which several gravestones are still found. Tradition speaks of the house and shop now in the occupation of Mr. Walsh, butcher, Main street, as having formerly been a Roman Catholic establishment. The Primitive Methodists and Christian Brethren have chapels also in the town. The population has considerably increased during the last thirty years. Old people are still living who can remember the town being little more than a moderately sized village. Bingley is larger now than Bradford was in 1821, the population of the latter place then being only 13,064. In 1801, Bingley township included 4100 souls; in 1821, 6136; in 1831, 8036; in 1841, 10,157; in 1851,

another illustration of those well known words, "God made the country, and man made the town."

It is a place, however, of some antiquity. William the Conqueror gave the lordship of Bingley to Erneis de Berun. In the twelfth year of the reign of King John, William de Gant held a charter for a market here. The cross and market-house bear the marks of great antiquity, and evidently show that as a market town it has at one time been a place of considerable importance. In 1621 a castle stood on what is called Bailey hill. In 1668 the manor was in the possession of Robert Benson, Esq., whose son was created the first lord Bingley. At the siege of Bradford the Bingley club-men rendered effective service on the side of the parliamentarians, and the army of General Fairfax encamped in this immediate neighbourhood. The church, a plain and ancient structure, was restored in the reign of Henry VIII, and in the same reign the free grammar school was founded. The Independents have long had a cause here. Oliver Heywood, one of the ejected ministers, originated a church shortly after his separation from the church of England, which has continued ever since. The old place of worship in Chapel lane, now occupied as dwelling-houses, was erected towards the end of the seventeenth century, and Accepted Lister, a noted preacher of his day, was the minister from 1695 to 1702. The Baptist chapel was erected in 1760, and has been subsequently enlarged. The Quakers had formerly a meeting house at Crossflatts, but their Society becoming extinct in this neighbourhood, the building has been turned into cottages. The burial ground adjoining is now used as garden allotments, in which several gravestones are still found. Tradition speaks of the house and shop now in the occupation of Mr. Walsh, butcher, Main street, as having formerly been a Roman Catholic establishment. The Primitive Methodists and Christian Brethren have chapels also in the town. The population has considerably increased during the last thirty years. Old people are still living who can remember the town being little more than a moderately sized village. Bingley is larger now than Bradford was in 1821, the population of the latter place then being only 13,064. In 1801, Bingley township included 4100 souls; in 1821, 6136; in 1831, 8036; in 1841, 10,157; in 1851,

13,434; and in 1861, 13,249. In 1600 a weekly assessment was made for the pensioning of wounded soldiers. A few items will show the relative wealth and populations of a few of the towns around: Bradford, 9d.; Wakefield, 10d.; Halifax, 8d.; Dewsbury, 6d.; Leeds, 10d.; Bingley, 8d.; Keighley, 8d.

As it is not the writer's intention to produce a history of Bingley, but to sketch the rise and progress of Methodism therein, he will content himself with the brief outline which he has given, and proceed at once with the subject he has taken in hand.

The introduction of Methodism into Bingley at a very early period was, doubtless, owing to its contiguity to Haworth, where the Rev. Wm. Grimshaw lived and laboured. The district for many miles round was visited by that devoted and laborious clergyman, whose earnest zeal and faithful preaching proved the means of awakening many to a sense of their spiritual condition, and of turning multitudes of the most ignorant and vile from darkness to light, and from the power of Satan unto God. Other zealous men were associated with him in this blessed work, such as John Nelson, William

Darney, Thomas Colbeck, Jonathan Maskew, Thomas Mitchell, Paul Greenwood and others; these itinerated the West Riding of Yorkshire, and broke up the fallow ground before the Wesleys visited this neighbourhood. William Darney was a native of Scotland, and one of the first race of Methodist preachers, having commenced his ministerial career as early as 1742. He was a man of unwearied toil and honest heart. Mr. Wesley held him in great esteem, and familiarly called him Scotch Willie. The common people, amongst whom he was exceedingly popular, used to call him Scotch Will. He visited these parts, and laboured with immense success. Grimshaw heard him on one of his visits, and felt the quickening power of his words, soon after which they joined together in conducting out of door services, when the rabble shouted, "Mad Grimshaw has turned Scotch Will's clerk."

Darney was a tall and strongly built man, with a loud shrill voice, and, when he choose, could assume a terrific countenance. One day when riding through the streets of Alnwick, a company of strolling players, who were lounging on the outside of their booth, recognised him;

he overheard them saying, "Here's Scotch Will, let's mob him." The horse on which he rode was a spirited one, and, putting it upon its mettle with spur and whip until it stood upon its hind legs, Darney rode up to them, and elevating his arm at the same time, cried out with a voice of thunder, "Ye sons of Belial, come on!" The men quailed before him, and begged his pardon. Numerous classes were raised, and little churches formed in the towns and villages around, which went by the name of "William Darney's societies." These were all placed under the pastoral oversight and care of Mr. Grimshaw, and formed what was commonly known as "Grimshaw's round." It is certain that Darney itinerated this neighbourhood prior to 1751, for in that year he published a volume of hymns, in one of which he recounts his adventures and the reception he met with in the places where he laboured. Bingley is not mentioned in the list, which is somewhat strange, as the size of the town and the extent of the population exceeded other places in the locality which he visited. Possibly he might have preached here without anything transpiring to kindle his poetic fire. As some of the verses refer to places in this neighbourhood, we will quote a few, the doggerel rhyme of which must be passed over for the sake of the information they contain. We make the extract from an original copy of the hymns.

In *Leedes*, and many Towns around,
The work goes sweetly on ;
There's many hear the Gospel Sound,
And to the Saviour turn.

On *Bradford* likewise look thou down,
Where Satan keeps his Seat ;
Come by thy Power, Lord him dethrone,
For thou art very great.

In *Windall*, and in *Baildon* Town,
Thy children simple be :
In *Yeadon*, and in *Menston Green*,
Some truly mourn for thee.

In *Ecclesall*, they're stiff and proud,
And few that dwell therein
Do shew they've any fear of God,
Or hatred unto sin.

O let them feel thy mighty Power,
Before that they do die ;

And save them from their hellish Gore,
On Jesus to rely.

In *Keighley*, by thy own right Hand,
A Church is planted there;
O help them Saviour all to stand,
Thy goodness to declare.

Haworth's a Place that God doth own,
With many a sweet smile;
With Power the Gospel's preach'd therein,
Which many one doth feel.

At *Bradford* dale, and *Thornton* Town,
And Places all around;
And at *Lingbob* sometimes at Noon,
The Gospel trump we sound.

He thus goes on describing various places in the kingdom, extending his long hymn to 104 verses.

Previous to Darney's visits to this neighbourhood, a great religious awakening had taken place, during which Bingley shared in the Pentecostal visitation. This occurred about 1744, and very soon afterwards the Bingley society was first formed. It was, probably, in this revival that Jonathan Maskew was converted.

He was a native of this parish, and one of the first Methodists in these parts. He began to preach soon after his conversion, and was recognised by Mr. Wesley as a travelling preacher in 1752. For some years he lived in Mr Grimshaw's family, and accompanied him on many of his preaching tours. He was a zealous and warm-hearted evangelist, and endured much persecution in his work. At Guiseley, he was stripped naked, rolled in the dirt, and deprived almost of life by his brutal persecutors. His preaching was attended with great power. Mr. Wesley said of him, "Ten such preachers as Jonathan Maskew would carry the world before them." He died a happy death in 1793, aged 82. It is an interesting fact for the Bingley Methodists to know that such a man was born within the limits of their parish. Jonathan Maskew and Wm. Darney's names appear often upon the pages of the old circuit book. The following are some of the items, which will no doubt provoke a smile amongst modern Methodists. "A pair of boots for Wm. Darney 14s." "Paid for Jonathan Maskew's shirts and stockings, 14s. 10d." "To Jonathan Maskew's hat, 5s." "To two shirts for Jonathan Maskew, 13s. ;

to three cravats for ditto, 3s.; to pumps, 6s.; to stockings, 3s. 6d." "To Jonathan Maskew's coat, £1. 12s. 6d. ; to Wm. Parker for Jonathan Maskew's stocks, 4s. 9d.; to Jonathan Maskew's coat making, 4s. 6d. ; to do. for garnish, 7s.6d."

Somewhere about the same time, Thomas Lee, or Tommy Lee, as he was commonly called, another of the early preachers, was instrumental in turning many to the Lord about here. In his autobiography, he says, "About this time I was invited to Harden Moor, Lingbobin, near Wilsden, and Thornton, above Bradforth; as these were places where no one had preached yet, I thought, if God would own me here, and raise up a people for himself, I shall know that he hath sent me. He did so, many found peace with God, and a society was raised in each place." It is evident from this that Methodism gained an early footing in Wilsden and Harden. The Lingbob services mentioned both by Darney and Lee resulted in the formation of a society, which continued for some time, and then became extinct. In 1760 the quarterage of this place was ten shillings. Those converted at Harden were identified with the society at Bingley.

Amongst those brought to the knowledge of

the truth about this time was another Bingley man, who lived to win for himself in the Methodist world an honourable name; we allude to Thomas Mitchell. Early in life he became a soldier, and served in the Yorkshire Blues during the Scotch Rebellion. After his discharge he gave himself to the Lord, and, in 1748, entered the Methodist ministry, in which he laboured with great usefulness for nearly forty years. He was a man of limited talents as a preacher, but by the simplicity of his manners, and entire devotedness to the one great business of saving souls, he was rendered extensively useful. The persecution he met with was of the most brutal kind. We will give one instance, which for fiendish cruelty has seldom been surpassed. It occured in Lincolnshire. He says, "On Sunday, August 7th, 1751, I came to Wrangle very early in the morning; I preached as usual at five, about six, two constables came at the head of a large mob. They violently broke in upon the people, seized upon me, pulled me down, and took me to a public house, where they kept me till four in the afternoon. Then one of the constables seemed to relent, and said, 'I will go to the minister and enquire of him whether we may not now let the poor man go.' When he came back, he said, 'They were not to let him go yet.' So he took me out to the mob, who presently hurried me away, and threw me into a pool of standing water. It took me up to the neck. Several times I strove to get out, but they pitched me in again. They told me I must go through it seven times. I did so, and then they let me come out. When I had got on dry ground, a man stood ready with a pot of white paint. He painted me all over from head to foot; and then they carried me into the public house again. Here I was kept until they put five more of the friends into the water. Then they came and took me out again, and carried me to a great pond, which was railed in on every side, being ten or twelve feet deep. Here, four men took me by the legs and arms, and swung me backwards and forwards. For a moment I felt the flesh shrink; but it was quickly gone. I gave myself up to the Lord, and was content his will should be done. They swung me two or three times, and then threw me as far as they could into the water. The fall and the water soon took away my senses, so that I felt nothing more. But some of them were not willing to have me drowned, so they watched till I came above water, and then catching hold of my clothes with a long pole, made shift to drag me out." After describing further indignities which he suffered, he goes on to say, "Some of the mob then went to the minister again to know what they must do with me. He told them, 'You must take him out of the parish.' So they came and took me out of bed a second time. But I had no clothes to put on, my own being wet, and also covered with paint. But they put an old coat about me, took me about a mile and set me upon a little hill. They then shouted three times, 'God save the king, and the devil take the preacher!'"

Thomas Mitchell, before he became a preacher, removed to Bradford, and at one time was a solitary Methodist in that town. He says, "Mr. John Wesley came to Bradford (1747) and preached on, 'This one thing I do.' He joined several of us in class which met about a mile from the town. But all of them fell back and left me alone." When we look at Methodism in Bradford at the present, and contrast it with the day when Thomas Mitchell stood alone, we may well exclaim, "What hath God wrought!" All

B

honour to the name of that good man who remained faithful amongst the faithless, and Bingley Methodists may feel no small measure of gratification in the fact that he was born in their parish, and sprung from their soil. The early notices of deceased ministers in the Conference records were very brief, but expressive. John Fletcher occupies a single line, and Charles Wesley only about six lines. In the minutes of 1785 it is asked, "Who has died this year?" Answer, "Thomas Mitchell an old soldier of Jesus Christ."

In the year 1757, Mr. Wesley paid his first visit to Bingley. The work of God was chiefly conducted up to this time by Grimshaw and his zealous helpers. The societies formed by these good men were brought into connexion with the United Societies, as the Methodists were first called, and placed under the authority and supervision of the founder of Methodism. In the first notice of Bingley in his Journal, he says, "Sat. May 21.—I had a little conference with our preachers (at Keighley.) In the afternoon I preached at Bingley. I have not lately seen so genteel a congregation; yet the word of God fell heavy upon them." He remained all night in the town, and, after preaching at five o'clock on Sunday morning, "took horse for Haworth." This record, however complimentary it may be to the respectability of his hearers, does not say much in favour of their religious condition. On the same page of the Journal he alludes to an earthquake which had recently shook an extensive part of Yorkshire and Lancashire. He writes, "Here (Haslingden) I learned that the earthquake observed near Heptonstal, had been sensibly felt by very many persons from Bingley." It would appear from this that his informants were Bingley people, and that there were " many" of them. Probably numbers from this town had gone into Lancashire to hear him preach, and while there gave him an account of what was felt of the shock about here, as well as invited him to this place, which he visited two or three days afterwards.

His second visit was in 1761, respecting which he simply writes, "July 8, I rode to Knaresborough. The remaining part of the week I preached at Guiseley, Bingley, and Keighley." In 1766 he came again, and sorrowfully writes, "Aug. 4, Monday.—At one I preached at Bingley, but with an heavy heart, finding so many of the Methodists here, as well as at Haworth, perverted by the Anabaptists. I see clearer and clearer none will keep to us unless they keep to the Church. Whosoever separate from the Church will separate from the Methodists." It must be borne in mind that Mr. Wesley was strongly attached to the Church of England, in which he had been brought up, and of which he was an ordained minister. When he commenced his itinerant career he never contemplated a separation from its communion, but was greatly opposed to it, and constantly warned the people against it. His great object at the first was to promote a revival of religion in the Church, and not to create a religious community outside of it. Subsequently his views on this matter underwent material alteration. The great head of the church showed him that there were vaster designs to accomplish than limiting his labours within the pale of the Establishment, and, whilst persecution thrust him out of the church of his choice, providence opened before him wider fields of usefulness, and taught him that, whatever might be his own ecclesiastical predilections, God intended him to feel, what he afterwards so nobly expressed in those well known words,

"The world is my parish." These sentiments which he entertained at the beginning of his mission, will account for the strong expression he used in describing the secession of several members of society at Bingley. The Baptists were dissenters, and dissent was offensive to Church of Englandism then, as well as at the present time. It is likely, however, that those who left the Methodist society did so on conscientious grounds, preferring Non-conformity and Independency to modes of worship as by law established, to which Mr. Wesley in that day rigidly adhered. Local tradition states that a division in the Methodist society here took place about the time mentioned by Mr. Wesley, and that a considerable number left and originated the Baptist church in this town. Amongst the seceders was a Mr. John Skirrow, a zealous and useful local preacher, who became one of the principal supporters of the Baptist interest in this locality. He died in 1785, in the 75th year of his age, and was interred in the Baptist chapel, Bingley. From Mr. Wesley's words the secession appears to have been on a large scale, for he speaks of "many" having left; implying that before the separation the society was somewhat numerous. It is not certain when the division actually occurred, but it must have transpired between the years 1760 and 1766. In the year 1763 the Bingley society numbered about thirty members. The following list of their names, residences, and social positions, will no doubt prove interesting.

CLASS, No. 1.

Thomas Middlesbrough,	Farmer,	Castlefield. Leader.
John Wildman,	Plasterer,	Bingley.
Benjamin Wilkinson,	Husbandman,	Micklewood.
John Gott,	Cordwainer,	Bingley.
James Farrah,	Old man,	,,
Sarah Moor,	Spinner,	Woodside.
John Gott	Stuff maker,	Bingley

CLASS, No. 2.

John Curtiss,	Stuff maker,	Bingley, Leader.
Martha Curtiss,	,,	,,
Wm. Maud,	Husbandman,	,,
Wm. Whitley,	Tailor,	,,
James Whitley,	,,	,,
John Whitaker,	Stuff maker,	Harden.
Mary Whitaker,	,,	,,
William Haughton,	Weaver,	Micklewood.

Sarah Harrison,	Spinner,	Bingley.
Thos. Patrick,	Weaver,	,,
Robt Watson,	Gentleman,	Beck.
Ann Dobson,	Glazier,	,,
Abraham Hartley,	Labourer,	Common.

CLASS, No. 3.

David Binns,	Weaver,	Harden brow, Leader
Joseph Brown,	Cordwainer,	,,
John Jackson,	Weaver,	,,
Christian Townend,	,,	,,
Abrm. Mitchell,	Woolcomber,	,,
Grace ————	Spinner,	
Eliz. Wood,	Servant,	
Robt. Walsh,	Weaver,	
Mary Middlesbrough,	Yeoman,	
Hanh. Wild,	Spinner,	
John Walker,	Shop-keeper,	
John Whitley,	Farmer,	

Some of these lived long enough to be known by persons who are alive at the present time. Benny Wilkinson was a well-known character. He was a simple-hearted, zealous, and good old pilgrim, and although greatly esteemed, was suffered to end his days in the workhouse, a fact not very creditable to the Methodists of that day. At his death the streets were crowded to witness his funeral, and the singers of the chapel sang a solemn hymn from the doors of the old Poor house in Myrtle-place down to the church gates. Poor old Benny! men placed thy body in a paupers grave, but, like thy prototype of want, angels carried thee to Abraham's bosom. Nanny Wood who is now in her 88th year, is fond of telling how, when a girl, she fell into the river Aire, and was carried down by the stream, and how Benny plunged in after her, and caught her by the little finger just as she was sinking to the bottom.

The various callings appended to the members' names show that spinning and weaving a century ago was the principal occupation of the labouring classes. But what a change a hundred years have wrought! There were no tall chimneys then, nor rattling machinery, nor crowded mills, but with slow and patient strokes the weaver drove the shuttle through his loom. Men as well as things have changed, some for the better, others for the worse. In manufacture, agriculture, commerce, education, modes of travelling, and the condition of the labouring classes, in all these wonderful advancements have been made, yet it is to be feared that the robust and earnest piety of God's people in that day, is wanting in the present race of christians. The thirty-two members just enumerated formed the Methodist church in Bingley in 1763. The cause was no doubt shattered and broken by the division which occurred. Pecuniary difficulties came early upon them, and they were compelled to petition the Conference for assistance. In the minutes for 1766, we find, under the question, "What places petition for help?" amongst other towns, Bingley is named as receiving £5. The Conference this year was held at Leeds, and commenced a few days after Mr. Wesley had been here, and it is reasonable to suppose that the sorrow he felt on account of the havoc which had been made would lead him to sympathise with this application, and to grant the help they sought. Various sums were afterwards granted; in 1769, £10.; in 1770, £6. 6s. 2d.; in 1772, £2. 10s.; and in 1775, £24. It is a matter of conjecture as to what occasioned their necessities, and why they required help. They had no chapel debt upon their shoulders, for the old chapel was not built until some time after these grants were made. It is probable, however, that lodgings were provided for the preachers, the members generally being too poor to accommodate them during their visits, and to assist them in meeting these expenses those sums were given.*

Very little seems to be known by the present race of Methodists in Bingley, respecting the previous places of worship used by their forefathers. The writer has been at considerable pains to find out where they formerly worshipped. It appears that the first place was a blacksmith's shop which stood on Elm tree hill, near to the entrance of what is now called Gott's yard. Mr. Hodgson of Crossflatts states that he has heard his grandfather often speak of having preached there. The next place was a large room over a block of buildings which occupied the site where the first chapel was erected. It was related by the late David Walbank, a well-known old Methodist, that, while fitting up this

---

* Mary Wilkinson states that her great grandfather, Jonathan Gott, a cordwainer, lived in a house under the preaching room, prior to the building of the first chapel, and that he had a room of his house set apart expressly for the use of the preachers when they came to this town.

room, he overheard some of the members expressing great anxiety as to how the rent was to be raised, which only amounted to thirty shillings a year. In this room Methodism seems to have prospered, for we find after a few years occupation, that the property was purchased, and the whole turned into a chapel. At what precise date this took place it is difficult to say, the deeds and documents having passed out of the hands of the Methodists when the building was sold. In Myles' History of Methodism, published in 1813, there is a list of all the chapels in the kingdom, and the dates when they were erected. Bingley is put down as being built in 1770. This must refer to the Room, and cannot apply to the Chapel, for the writer has conversed with two or three old people upwards of 80 years of age, who remember the chapel being built, but cannot recollect the year. Myles' date would make it 93 years ago, and, consequently, beyond the recollection of the individuals referred to* This old sanctuary is

---

* Since the above was written a few additional particulars have been obtained. The date of its erection must have been two or three years prior to 1795. A painful incident which occurred in that year has helped us to this conclusion. Nearly seventy years ago a person named

spoken of by aged members, as having been a very commodious and comfortable place of worship, and some of them do not hesitate to express their preference to it over the present chapel. Old and hallowed associations will no doubt bind their hearts to the former temple, where some of their best religious friendships were formed, and the most precious manifestations of God's power and love were realised.

Walker Waddington was bitten by a mad dog, and soon afterwards was seized with hydrophobia while attending divine service in the Wesleyan chapel. The scene is described as one of intense and painful excitement. Suddenly rising from his seat in the midst of the congregation, the poor man endeavoured to lay hold of a large chandelier which hung suspended from the roof in the centre of the chapel, exclaiming vehemently as he did so, "Put out those lights! put out those lights!" Consternation and terror spread through the audience, and a painful sensation was felt throughout the town. He was conducted to his home as speedily as possible, where shortly after he expired. It is commonly reported that his death was hastened by suffocation, a statement which we cannot credit. His death took place September the 1st, 1795, aged 31. William Briggs of this town states that he was present at the time of the above-named occurrence, when a boy along with his mother, and distinctly recollects that the chapel had been built but a short time before. Other statements from aged persons fix its erection about the same time. It is a question whether a slight mistake was not made in Myles' list by printing the year 1770 instead of 1790.

Making allowances for the prejudices, and attachment to old places, which elderly persons are always fond of entertaining, there is no doubt but that God did abundantly bless his cause and people in that old Methodist chapel. The entire building has been turned into shops and dwelling-houses. That part now in the occupation of Mr. Christopher Foster, was formerly the residence of the minister, which entered by a private door into the chapel. There was a side entrance on Elm tree hill, and another in Main street, the principal one being in the front near the Market-house. The stone at the Main street doorway is much worn. Many a pilgrim's foot which crossed that threshold is now where the wicked cease from troubling, and the weary are at rest. The old pulpit, which was formerly supported by a large stone pillar, is now used for week-night service in the room underneath the present chapel. The property was purchased by the late Mr. Thos. Whitley for £800., and put into the condition in which it is found at present. The following individuals were trustees at the time the place was sold, in 1817, John Moorhouse, Joshua Briggs, Joseph Cryer, John Dean, Matthew Foster, William Whitley, William

Foulds, John Wild, David Binns, Joseph Barraclough, and Thomas Nicholson. The Bingley society was at first included in the Haworth circuit, which extended as far as Whitehaven. Circuits in that day embraced several counties. At the Conference of 1746 it was asked, "How are our Circuits now divided?" and the answer was, "Yorkshire, (including Cheshire, Lancashire, Derbyshire, Nottinghamshire, Rutlandshire, Lincolnshire.)" In 1749 Haworth was the head of the Circuit, no doubt on account of Mr. Grimshaw residing there, and continued such until 1776, when Keighley took its place, and appears on the minutes of that year for the first time. In olden times these Circuits, or "Rounds," as they were often called, were extensive spheres of labour, involving weary journeys and long absences from home, and required of the preachers many sacrifices of personal and domestic comfort, beside the fierce persecution which they had to endure. But God raised up men fitted for the work, men of deep piety, earnest zeal, strong faith, and fervent prayer, who, although not highly educated, yet were mighty in the scriptures, and full of compassion for the souls of men. And it was by such devoted messengers of the churches, with God's blessing on their labours, that Methodism was built upon foundations which a century of trial and persecution has not been able to remove. Methodism in olden times was a very different affair compared with what it is in the present day, not in its great doctrines and principles, they remain unaltered, but in the circumstances both of its ministers and people. Christopher Hopper said in his day, "I had to ride sixteen miles before I met with another Methodist, and he was in a *cellar* at Rochdale; then I rode eleven miles before I met with another, and he was in a *garret* at Manchester." The condition of Wesleyan ministers as regards their pecuniary resources has also undergone a great improvement since the time when the book of a certain circuit received the following item, "For turning and altering the superintendent's coat, and making it fit his colleague, 7s.;" or, when Bradford in 1770 allowed its ministers the following stipend. "The preacher's weekly board, 13 weeks at 3s. 6d. per week, £2. 5s. 6d. Quarterage £3.; ditto for wife, £1. 17s. 6d.; allowed for servant, 12s. 6d.; ditto for turnpikes, 6s.; Total £8. 1s. 6d.!!" The preachers are better cared for now, and are not often obliged to go through a scene like the following. A half starved preacher once applied to his steward for his salary. The steward began to lecture him about his anxiety for money, saying, he thought he preached for souls. "Souls," said the poor fellow, "I can't eat souls, and if I could, a thousand such as yours would not make a decent meal."

One of the early Methodists in this locality was a Mr. John Whitley of Eldwick Cragg. He was led by a course of singular providences to take a farm at that place. On his arrival, he found the residence not ready for occupation, and therefore took lodgings for a while at a neighbour's house. In this house the Methodists were accustomed to preach the word of life, and it was on one of those occasions, under a sermon by Mr. John Skirrow, that Mr. Whitley and his wife were both awakened, and ultimately became steady and consistent members. He became a useful local preacher until 1774, when he was called into the full work of the ministry, in which he continued until 1779, when he retired back again into private life. When Mr. Wesley urged him to enter the itinerant work he declined, saying, "I have only two sermons, sir, what am I to do?" Mr. Wesley replied, "God that has enabled you to preach two, can give you ability to preach two thousand."

Francis, son of the above, also became a zealous Methodist. His conversion was somewhat singular. He was present when his father and mother were awakened, but the sermon does not appear to have affected his heart. For some time he entertained feelings hostile to religion. In 1769 he married, and soon afterwards his wife was converted to God. Francis became a persecutor of God's people, and one day when his wife had retired into an out-house to pray, he violently pushed the door upon her, with the design of provoking her to anger, and getting her to give up her religion. But the meek and christian spirit with which she received his unkindness moved his heart. He was brought under the most distressing convictions, and drank deeply of the wormwood and the gall. He found mercy, gave himself to the Lord, became a zealous local preacher, and for many years stood as a pillar in the church. He was a man of great punctuality in all things. It is said that he never, on any account, missed a

c

single appointment to preach: and for fifty-two years he was absent from his class *only three times*. He finished his course in 1821, greatly respected, aged 77. A tombstone in Bingley church yard bears the following inscription:

" SACRED TO THE MEMORY "
Of Martha, wife of John Whitley, who departed this life in peace, February 20, 1776, aged 58. Also of the said John Whitley, who died in London, March 11, 1813, aged 90. Of Sarah, wife of their son, Francis Whitley, who died September 18th, 1815, aged 73. And of the said Francis Whitley, who was 52 years a member of the Methodist Society, 48 of which he had been a distinguished local preacher. He closed a useful life in peace, November 27, 1821, aged 77."

Francis succeeded his father on the farm when the latter entered the ministry. The house stands on the right hand side of the road between the Beck and the Cragg, and close to the footpath which leads from the former to the latter place. Many hallowed associations cling to that old farm house. No doubt Mr. Wesley and the early preachers often called there on their way from Otley to Bingley. Many a hymn of praise has there been sung, and many a wayworn and weary preacher has found rest and hospitality beneath its roof. One of the daughters of Francis Whitley became the mother of John Nicholson, the Airedale poet. When but eight years old Nicholson wrote rhyme. It appears that his grandfather had two neighbours which greatly annoyed him, and one day when about that age, the young poet wrote upon the barn door the following verse:

> "Good God of truth, take Mat and Ruth,
> Unto thy heavenly throne.
> Then good old Frank may live in crank,
> And be disturbed by none."

We will now resume our quotations from Mr. Wesley's Journal. In 1770, he was again at Bingley, but simply writes, "July, Monday and Tuesday, I preached at Bingley and Bradford." In 1772, he says, "Monday, July 6, at noon I preached to a large congregation at Bingley." In May, 1774, he paid another flying visit, and writes, "On Monday, Tuesday, and Wednesday, I preached at Bingley and Yeadon." In 1776, he was here again, and writes, "Saturday, May 27, I preached in the Church at Bingley, perhaps not so filled before for these hundred years." God gave him favour with the people here, and crowds always flocked to hear him. Saturday or Monday, at noon or early morning, multitudes hastened to catch instruction from his lips. The enthusiastic and respectful welcome which Bingley gave him speaks well for the inhabitants, and contrasts favourably with the brutal treatment which he met with in other places. In 1779, he was again here, and says, "Monday, April 19, I preached in Bingley Church to a numerous congregation. I dined with Mr. Busfeild in his little paradise; but it can give no happiness unless God is there." This is an interesting paragraph. The place alluded to was the mansion now called Myrtle Grove, then in the possession of Johnson Atkinson Busfeild, Esq., grandfather of the present Wm. Ferrand, Esq., of Harden Grange. In the hands of Mr. Busfeild the place underwent a thorough transformation, and, from a large farm house known as Spring Head, it rose into the beautiful residence which Mr. Wesley designated "a little paradise." The father and mother of Mr. Michael Speight lived with Mr. Busfeild many years, the former as coachman and the latter as cook. Mr. Speight has heard his parents speak of Mr. Wesley's visits up at the Grove. Mr. Busfeild was a kind-hearted, gentlemanly man, and, withal, fond of a little humour. It is related that one Sunday morning while at church, the congregation was greatly alarmed by an earthquake which shook the building, when Benjamin Ferrand, Esq., said to Mr. Busfeild, "We had nearly all gone down together this morning." Mrs. Busfeild, who was leaning on the arm of her husband replied, "I hope not, the rich and the poor would surely not have gone to the same place." "No, my dear," said Mr. Busfeild, "I'm afraid the rich would have but little chance of that." On one occasion when the Methodists were having a great revival, and in their prayer meetings were more noisy than usual, a gentleman who lived near the chapel was greatly annoyed and alarmed at their proceedings, and, supposing a riot had taken place, he hastened up to Mr. Busfeild and urged him, as a magistrate, to go down and quell it. Mr. B. went down, walked through the preacher's house into the chapel, and, perceiving what was going on, said, "Go on, go on, you cannot do better." It is said that Mr. Wesley once gave a severe reproof to the above-named Benjamin Ferrand, Esq. When the reverend gentleman was preaching in the church the latter gave way to immoderate laughter, which greatly disconcerted the preacher. Mr. Wesley paused, and fixing his eye upon the offender, said, "I regard the sneer of a mortal no more than the laugh of a monkey," or words to that effect. Mr. Ferrand afterwards admitted that the preacher was right, and the rebuke was well merited.

In 1780, Mr. Wesley was here again. He writes, "Sunday, April 23, Mr. Richardson being unwilling that I should preach any more in Haworth church, Providence opened another; I preached in Bingley church, both morning and afternoon. This is considerably larger than the other. It rained hard in the morning, this hindered many; so that those who did come got in pretty well in the forenoon, but in the afternoon very many were obliged to go away." While the church of his old and departed friend, Mr. Grimshaw, was closed against him, that of Bingley continued at his service. The vicar of the parish at the time was the Rev. Richard Hartley, father of the late Dr. Hartley. He entered upon the living in 1741, and held it forty-eight years, dying in 1789. His was a brave and pious heart which prompted him, amidst reproach and persecution, to give the right hand of fellowship to the despised servants of the Lord, and to wish them God speed. In 1782 Mr. W. came again, and says, "Sunday, May 28, Bingley church was hot, but the heat was supportable, both morning and afternoon." The next entry is a very interesting one, it occurred in 1784. He says, "Thursday, July 15, I retired to Otley and rested two days. Sunday, 18th, I preached morning and afternoon in Bingley church. Before service, I stepped into the Sunday school, which contains two hundred and forty children, taught every Sunday by several masters, and superintended by the curate. So many children in one parish are restrained from open sin, and taught a little good manners at least, as well as to read the Bible. I find these schools springing up whereever I go. Perhaps God may have a deeper end therein than men are aware of. Who knows but some of these schools may become nurseries for christians. Tuesday, 20th, Though it rained hard all day, in the morning we had a good congregation at five. Wednesday, 21. I met the society and found but one or two of the original members, most of them having gone to

Abraham's bosom. I was a little surprised to find that only two or three of the rest had stood fast in the glorious liberty. But, indeed, most of them recovered their loss some years ago. Thursday, 22. Although it rained, yet I met the congregation, and most of them were athirst for salvation. Friday, 23. Abundance of people were present at five in the morning, and such a company of children as I have hardly seen in England." From this long extract it appears he remained in Bingley nearly a week, a very unusual circumstance. It might be supposed at first that there was some mistake in the Journal, but several things concur to render his week's sojourn here probable. He was at the time in his 81st year, and bodily infirmities were beginning to come upon him. Then we find him resting two days at Otley before coming here, which indicates that repose was necessary. The observations also which he makes respecting the great number of children attending the Friday morning service evidently refer to the same which he visited on the previous Sabbath. In addition to these, we may suppose that the kind and hospitable entertainment which he would no doubt meet with at the "little paradise" up at Myrtle Grove, as well as the open doors of the church, and free access, to the pulpit at all times, these things make it probable that this town once had the privilege and honour of entertaining for a week the founder of Methodism. His remarks about the Sabbath school are interesting. About this time Sunday schools began to be formed in different parts of the kingdom, chiefly through the labours of Robert Raikes, Esq., of Gloucester, and Bingley has the credit of being amongst the first established. The writer has been favoured with an inspection of the original rules and regulations of the school in this town, a few items from which will prove interesting to the friends of Sunday schools. The date of its foundation is June, 1784, just one month before Mr. Wesley visited it. All subscribers of five shillings were to be "Governors" for the year. Mr. John White was elected "Upper Master," with a stipend of half-a-crown a day, and Mr. Jeremiah Briggs to be "Under Master" at two shillings per day; John Longbottom and Solomon Clark, "Assistant Masters," at a shilling per day. The school hours to be from eight in the morning until six in the evening from the first of April until the first of October; and from nine to four during the winter. Amongst other regulations we observe the following, "The children of Dissenters to be allowed to attend their own places of worship." "All parents receiving parish relief to be compelled to send their children on pain of forfeiting such relief." "All persons having parish apprentices to be admonished to send them regularly at least one half of the day." The whole is closed with the following excellent clause, "That above all things, the masters take all proper occasion to plant the fear of God in their hearts, to make them serious and concerned for their souls, and to awaken them into a sense of the danger they are in without the grace of God, and the aid of religion." The subscriptions for the first year amounted to £47. 4s., and the expenditure to £39. 3s. 1½d. Bingley has done its part in Sunday school efforts in proportion to its population. Eighty years ago it started well, and in 1863, it is not weary in this sphere of well doing. The following are the numbers on the books of the various schools at the present time, 1863: the actual attendance will of course be less, but this return of those on the books will be fair to all parties.

Church of England - - - - - 326.
Independents - - - - - - - 258.
Baptists - - - - - - - - 114.
Primitive Methodists - - - - 282.
Christian Brethren - - - - - 124.
Wesleyan Methodists - - - - 456.

Total - - - - - 1560.

On turning again to Mr. Wesley's Journal we find he was here in 1786, when he writes, "Sunday, May 23. I preached in Haworth church in the morning, and Bingley church in the afternoon, but as there were many hundreds that could not get in, Mr. Atmore preached abroad at the same time." Mr. Atmore was one of the early preachers, and acquired a respectable position in the connexion; he published an interesting work called, "Memorials of Methodist Preachers." We next come to the record of his last visit, which took place in 1788, when he was fast drawing near to the close of his long and laborious life. He writes, "Sunday, May 27. I preached at Haworth church in the morning, crowded sufficiently, as was Bingley church in the afternoon; but, as many could not get in,

Mr. Wrigley preached to them in the street, so that they did not come in vain." Mr. Wrigley was then appointed to the Huddersfield circuit, and probably accompanied Mr. Wesley when in this locality. This occurred two years and ten months before he finished his course. What an impressive and interesting sight it must have been to see that venerable minister of Christ, in his EIGHTY-FIFTH year, pressing through the crowds which thronged to hear him, and hundreds unable to get into the church. Sometimes he preached out of doors, although we find no allusion to it in his Journals. Mr. Christopher Foster states that he has heard his father tell of hearing him preach on some steps which formerly stood near to where the Fleece Inn now stands, and the late Mr. Thomas Longbottom once heard him as he stood upon the "horsing steps" of the White Horse public house. Nanny Wood, who is fast verging towards ninety, has a distinct remembrance of seeing him when she was a girl, passing down the town in his gown and bands, whilst multitudes thronged the streets to see him, and such was the excitement which his presence occasioned that it was called reproachfully, "Wesley

Fair." His visits amounted altogether to thirteen, extending over a period of upwards of thirty years. The following is the order in which they took place :—

May,	1757.		April,	1779.
July,	1761.		April,	1780.
August,	1766.		May,	1782.
July,	1770.		July,	1784.
July,	1772.		May,	1786.
May,	1774.		May,	1788.
May,	1776.			

From this period Methodism seems to have moved onwards in the town without any particular incidents to mark its history. The society kept up its numbers, God owned his word, and, at various times, blessed out-pourings of the Spirit were vouchsafed. In 1790, the Rev. Isaac Lilly, a native of Bingley, commenced his ministerial career. He was a man of gentle and amiable disposition, and much beloved in the circuits where he laboured. His ministry was attended with divine unction, and his clear and practical preaching was rendered extensively useful. In 1820 he was compelled through mental and bodily infirmities to retire from the active work, and for several years was entirely confined to his bed. A few months, however, before his death he met with an accident, the sudden shock of which had the effect of restoring his reason, and he died in great peace in the 86th year of his age.

About this time Elizabeth Dickinson created considerable excitement in this neighbourhood by her open air preaching, as well as the "trances" which she professed to fall into. She was very young, being only about 19 years old, of unspotted reputation, with an ardent temperament, and great zeal in the cause of religion. Thousands flocked to hear her, and many were said to be converted through her instrumentality. Her so called trances were, doubtless, nothing more than vivid pictures of a wild and excited imagination, and visions of a brain evidently under the influence of some mental disturbance. She was attractive in person, and possessed a pleasing address, which no doubt contributed to her popularity. She was overtaken with her last illness when on a preaching visit at the house of a Mr. John Watson of Sandbeds, where she died, and was buried in Bingley churchyard in 1793, in the *twentieth* year of her age.

We pass over the next few years and come to the time when Bingley became the head of a circuit, which took place in 1808. Up to that year it had been connected with Keighley. At first it comprised what now form the Yeadon and Shipley circuits, as will be seen in the copy of a plan annexed, for 1812. Thornton, which was formerly in the Halifax circuit, and somewhere about 1824 was joined to Keighley, was included in the Bingley circuit until 1843, when it became connected with Great Horton. Cullingworth and Denholme were joined to Bingley in 1826. Yeadon was created a circuit in 1829, and Shipley in 1823: the latter was re-joined to Bingley in 1828, and separated again in 1830. The first ministers appointed to this circuit were the Rev. John Needham and the Rev. William Scholefield. The old plan will show the extent of the circuit and the amount of preaching each place had fifty years ago. Wilsden does not appear upon it, but stands upon the one immediately following, with preaching once a fortnight in the afternoon. Interesting sketches might be given of some of the men whose names appear in the list of preachers. All are dead but one, namely, No. 17. Mr. Shackleton is a

THE SUNDAY PLAN OF THE ITINERANT AND LOCAL PREACHERS, IN THE BINGLEY CIRCUIT.

1812-13.				AUGUST.				SEPTEMBER.				OCTOBER.				NOVEMBER.				DECEMBER.				JANUARY.				Explanation.
PLACES.	F.	A.	E.	2	9	16	23	30	6	13	20	27	4	11	18	25	1	8	15	22	29	6	13	20	27	3	10	17	24	31
Bingley	.. 9	1	6		4		2	s1		2		L1		2		1	2		s1	L2		1		2		1		1, 2,
Ditto	..	1		8	4	17		9		5		7	10		14	12		11		13	18		19		20		3	3, Whitley,
Ditto	..		6	3	6	17		2		1		2	1		2	1		2		1	2		1		2		1	4, Ackroyd, 5, Curtis,
Harden	.. 9			8		6		9		5		7	10		14	12		11		13	18		19		20		3	6, Bailey,
Gilstead	.. 9			20		7		3		6		8	9		5	4		10		11	12		14		18		8	7, Denison,
East-Morton	..	2		20		7		3		6		8	9		5	4		10		11	12		14		18		8	8, Coates, 9, Mellor,
Shipley	..10	2		3		8		2		L1		2	s1		2	1		2		1	L2		s1		2		1	10, Berry,
Ditto	..10	2			12		15	3		8		5	4		7	11		10		9	6		17		20			11, Fawthorp,
Heaton-Royds	2				3		7	17		19		18	13		10	9		8		20	14		12		15			12, Waterhouse, 13, Baldwin,
Cottingley	..		6		3		7	17		19		18	13		10	9		8		20	14		12		15			14, Sugden,
Baildon	..10	1½	5		7		1	2		s1		2	r.1		2	1		2		1	2		s1		L2			15, Holmes,
Ditto	..10	1¼		11		16		7		17		10	6		4	3		9		8	5		13		14		19	16, Whitaker, 17, Shackleton,
Yeadon	..10	2	5½	10		2		1		2		L1	2		s1	2		1		2	1		r.2		s1		2	18, Nicholson,
Ditto	..10	2		13		3		8		4		17	5			6		19	12	14		11		7		18		19, Hardacre,
Guiseley	.. 9			18		20		15		12		13	3			8		4		17	7		19		5		6	20, Nixon,

L, Lovefeast. S, Sacrament.

N.B.—QUARTERLY MEETING at YEADON, September 28; and at BINGLEY, December 28, to begin at 10 o'Clock.

supernumerary minister at present, residing in the Bedale circuit, and is upwards of ninety years of age. He is quite blind, but full of life and zeal in his Master's service. Another name will awaken mournful recollections, namely, No. 18, Nicholson. This was John Nicholson the Airedale poet. After he joined the Methodist society, he became a zealous and useful Sabbath school teacher, and, along with others, established schools at Eldwick and the Beck, which still continue. In 1812 his name appears upon the plan, having previously passed the usual period of probation. He was exceedingly popular as a preacher, and crowds flocked to hear him. His sermons were highly imaginative and interspersed with striking quotations from the sacred poets. The Rev. Alex Suter, the superintendent minister, took him by the hand with the intention of proposing him as a candidate for the Wesleyan ministry, but his marriage prevented this being carried out, and in 1815 he left the society, having no doubt previously lost his religion. His parents were consistent members of the Methodist society, his father being also a trustee of the chapel. As a poet he won for himself considerable fame; but his subsequent career and melancholy end have thrown a cloud over his memory and name. He perished in crossing the river Aire on the 13th of April, 1843, and was interred in Bingley churchyard, when a large concourse attended his funeral. A neat tombstone was erected by his widow, whom he left with eight children to mourn his unhappy fate. What distressing reflections does the history of poor Nicholson afford. The *son*, the *grandson*, and the *great grandson* of pious Wesleyans, and himself once a popular preacher of the gospel, yet pursuing a course, and meeting with a death, which his greatest admirers cannot but deplore.

About 1811 God was pleased to visit the society in this town with a gracious revival. Under the ministry of the Rev. A. Suter, and the Rev. R. Jackson, who were then in the circuit, many were converted and added to the church. One peculiarity which marked this revival was the great number of converts which had reached middle age and advanced periods of life, as well as the long and stedfast profession of many who were brought to God at the time, some of the fruits of that movement continuing even to this day. A singular circumstance occurred about this time to one William Hargreaves, a pious and devoted member of the Bingley society. He was called to pass through great domestic trials. He had seven sons, five of which enlisted into the army, and three fell in the service of their country. Fifteen years before his death he was visited with a severe illness, which, to all human appearance, was likely to prove fatal. While in this state it was powerfully impressed upon his mind that he would recover, and the words of Isaiah addressed to Hezekiah under similar circumstances, were applied with peculiar force to his mind: "I will add unto thy days fifteen years." He did recover and lived fifteen years longer. When in his last affliction, he told his friends that his allotted time had come, the fifteen years were expired, and he should have to die. This actually took place at the time indicated, exactly fifteen years from the previous illness in which the impression was made upon his mind. This is a remarkable fact, and is as authentic as it is remarkable. He died in 1810, aged 69.

About this time also departed this life, Mrs. Fell of Milner Field, an estimable and pious lady, and a true Methodist. For many years she walked with God, and adorned the religion of her Saviour in all things. She deeply sympathised with the poor around her, and was well known for her benevolence. Herself a widow, she felt for widows in their affliction. At Christmas she always sent seasonable presents to the necessitous. When her means were large, a fat beast was killed and distributed amongst the poorer tenants; when her circumstances became somewhat altered, a sheep was given in its place. The fine orchard and gardens at Milner Field yielded abundant fruit, and they were cultivated by this excellent woman principally for the sick and poor around her. Her name is almost forgotten among men, but her record is on high; and in the last grand adjudication of all things, she will receive the full reward of her doings from him who has said that a cup of cold water given to one of his disciples shall not go unrewarded. She died in 1811.

The Methodists of Bingley fifty or sixty years ago appear to have been a plain and earnest minded people, in their business transactions and social habits, as well as in their religion. There was less of the glitter and refinement of modern times it is true, but there was much steady principle and sterling worth amongst them. Some of their names are still held in great esteem not only by their descendants, but by the aged members of society who survive them. The writer has been deeply affected while listening to old members recounting the names of many who were the companions of their youth, and who took an active part in the affairs of Methodism in bygone times. He has caught hold of a few of those names, and has placed them on this page to preserve them from oblivion. Such as John and Nancy Horner, James and Susey Bentley, John Moorhouse, John Dean, David Walbank, James Speight, John Cryer, Samuel Curtiss, William Curtiss, William Cockshott; the last three were local preachers, and the last of the three was exceedingly popular on account of the extreme brevity of his sermons. Also John Longbottom, John Smith, John Wilkinson, shoe maker, Stephen Snowden, Matthew Longbottom, Thos. Longbottom (recently deceased), John Wild, shoe maker, David Binns,* John Wild of Castle

---

* Mr. Binns was a respectable woolstapler of this place, a plain and honest man, with the ring of the true metal about him. He was a

field, John Moore, John Wilkinson, chapel-keeper, Thomas Whitfield, John Heaton, Joseph Cryer, John Jackson, John Whitley, A. Ryecroft, Matthew Foster, William Foulds, and others. These in that day were the working-men of the society, and they evidently were working men, for their voices were heard in the prayer meetings, and their presence was seen in the love-feasts and band meetings constantly: and whilst many of them were poor, and others had their failings, yet, taken as a whole, they were "a band of men whose hearts God had touched," and men who laboured hard to promote the interests of the Redeemer's kingdom. Some of the wives of those whom we have named were good and godly women, and, along with their husbands, stood by the cause of Methodism through evil and good report.

---

steady and true-hearted Methodist, having his interest chiefly centred upon the chapel property, of which he was the steward, and towards the funds of which he was a liberal contributor. On his death-bed he sent for his successor, the late Mr. Isaac Smith, and committed into his hands the books, &c., after which he obtained a promise that the trust affairs should be taken care of: he then said, "There, I can now die happy." Mr. Smith efficiently performed the duties of this office, according to his promise, and has recently entered the spirit world.

In the year 1816 the present chapel was built. The circumstances which led to its erection were something like the following. The Wesleyans at that time were accustomed to conduct their Sabbath school tuition in the National school-room, in conjunction with the Church Sunday school. One of the regulations was that prayers at the opening and close of the school must be read. Some of the Methodist people feeling this to be a restraint upon their consciences, broke through the rule and offered extemporaneous prayer. This was forbidden; unpleasant feelings were awakened; and, finding union could no longer be continued on such terms, the Wesleyans resolved to build a school-room of their own. Steps were immediately taken, and a piece of land forming part of a croft belonging to Mr. John Dean was generously given for this object. After the school project was formed, several of the principal friends suggested that it would be better to build a new chapel on the same ground, and have the school-room underneath; a somewhat popular plan at that time. This suggestion was acted upon, and the building as it now stands was erected. The woodwork was done by Mr. John Dean, and the stonework by Messrs.

John and Jonathan Clark of this town. The total cost amounted to £3839. 10s. It is a substantial and well built chapel, perhaps larger than the population of that day required, the whole parish including then only about 6000 inhabitants, being less than half the present number. But the men who took it in hand evidently looked beyond the necessities of their own generation, and the increased prosperity and population of the neighbourhood have justified their expectations. It has been regretted by many that the front was not placed in an opposite direction to what it is; but it should be borne in mind that at the time of its erection scarcely a house stood betwixt it and the Dubb, so that instead of being hemmed in as at present, it commanded a good southerly prospect. Doctor Beaumont was appointed to the circuit the year after it was opened, and in a letter written by him at the time we learn his judgment of the place. He says, "The Bingley new chapel is an excellent place of worship, but built I think on a little too large a scale. The society in Bingley is however by no means in a flourishing condition, though in general our congregations are great, and the prospect before us encouraging." The form of the interior is not well arranged, the width being greater than the length, and the roof to the floor is inconveniently deep. The recent painting which it has undergone has given its interior a very neat appearance. During the first ten years the bottom was unpewed, but in 1827, the whole was filled with good useful pews at a cost of £115., which have been at various times improved. Six years after it was built the debt amounted to £2360., so that presuming no more money was raised between that time and the opening, we learn the amount actually realised when it was opened, namely, £1479.

The amount of seat rent was about £87. per annum, with £15. for rent of Sabbath school, and the annual interest on borrowed money amounted to £118. Various efforts to reduce the debt have been made at different times, and at present it amounts to £1395. Interest upon this sum has to be regularly paid by the trustees, which forms the strong reason why every seat-holder should be punctual in his payments, as well as that all who attend the chapel should assist in doing so, by taking seats when able. The trustees bear this responsibility for the benefit of the congregation, and they naturally look to the congregation for help and support. The first trustees were the following, namely, Thomas Whitley, Joshua Briggs, Joseph Cryer, David Binns, William Foulds, Matthew Foster, Joseph Barraclough John Dean, William Whitley, Thos. Nicholson (father of the poet), Jno. Sharp, E. Whitley, John Wilkinson, Thomas Longbottom.

One of the principal persons through whose instrumentality the present chapel was erected, was the late Mr. Thomas Whitley, who, along with his uncle the late Mr. Oliver, contributed largely towards the expenses. A few years after the chapel was completed Mr. Whitley built the two houses adjoining, and by deed made them over to the Wesleyan body in this town, subject to a rental of £21. per annum during his life, which was paid for a great number of years. One of these houses has been the residence of a minister from the first. The other minister's residence formerly stood near to where the railway bridge now crosses the road. It was taken down in 1847 to make way for the line which had to pass over its site. The Company granted a handsome compensation of £1000., as well as the old materials, a considerable part of which was used in the erection of the present minister's house in Cannon street.

It has been already stated that Dr. Beaumont was appointed to this circuit in 1817. Bingley was one of his earliest and happiest spheres of labour, and he ever cherished a pleasant remembrance of his sojourn here. His biographer says, "Bingley, near Bradford, was the next scene of his life. In this circuit he was especially useful and happy: indeed, his happiness seemed to be ever full, and yet ever increasing as the sphere of his labour enlarged. But against Bingley he placed a red letter in the name of friendship, as well as because of the productive sphere of labour which he found there, for there he met with friends for whom he always felt a strong affection, and in this scene of his early labours are his name and memory still precious and cherished." During his two years in this circuit he was made extensively useful, a great revival took place in the town society, and many were brought to God in various places. Ten years after his removal, when compelled by affliction to rest for awhile, he spent a considerable time at Gawthrop hall, near this place, where he was kindly entertained by Mr. and

Mrs. Thomas Whitley, who then resided there. This would prove no doubt a congenial spot to the Doctor. The old Manor house, built in the Tudor times, with its antique gables and numerous rooms, its thick walls and small diamond shaped window panes, hid in a quiet nook, and yet commanding a beautiful view of the valley of the Aire, would be an agreeable retreat to a man of Dr. Beaumont's tastes and temperament.

It was during the revival just named, under the joint ministry of Messrs. Blackett and Beaumont, that the late Rev. Wm. Longbottom, found peace and gave himself to the Lord. Mr. Longbottom was the son and grandson of eminently pious and devoted men. His grandfather, Matthew, was "a patriarchal, hoary-headed man, and a picture of happy, sanctified old age." His father, Thomas Longbottom, was a precious and blessed old saint. Everybody loved him, and in every house he found a welcome. Wicked men revered his presence, and little children rejoiced to see him in the streets; and all who knew him retain a pleasant remembrance of his name. He was a leader of five classes in the Bingley society, and after walking with God for sixty years, he died in peace on the 10th day of November, 1861, in the 83rd year of his age. The writer regrets that he had not the opportunity of a personal acquaintance with him before his departure to a better world; but the above sketch is the result of what he has gathered in conversation with various individuals respecting him.* William Longbottom, his son, entered

---

* After the above was written, a long and interesting account of his life and character was found in the *Airedale Courant*, which was prepared and read by the Rev. J. D. Julian, on the occasion of his preaching a funeral sermon for the deceased. We give a few extracts.

The following account is in his own hand-writing:

"A few of the first steps taken by Divine Providence and Grace towards the recovery of a poor sinner from the error of his ways.

"In the year 1801, I was then in the army, and the regiment was then stationed in Scotland, at Sterling, Falkirk, and Linlithgow. I was at the last mentioned place on a very fine Sunday in the month of July. We went to the Scotch Kirk in the forenoon. After dinner my comrade and myself agreed to have a walk. Just as we were going out of the house where we lodged, I took an old book off the shelf and slipped it under my coat, and we went into the fields and sat down under a hedge, when I took out the book and found the title "Christ's sure and certain coming to judgment." I read till we both trembled. I for one saw that all was wrong, and what to do to get saved I could not tell. I never had bowed my knees sincerely before the Lord, that I could think of, still I thought prayer was the only expedient. I felt determined not to retire to rest that night till I had attempted to pray

the Wesleyan ministry in 1827. In 1829, along with the Rev. Thomas Cryer, another Bingley youth, he took his departure for the East Indies, where he laboured with accept-

---

I wandered into the fields amongst the cows; I kneeled down and confessed my sins, and begged the Lord to have mercy on me. I had very confused views of the plan of salvation. I had frequently heard that Jesus Christ was the only refuge for a sinner, I therefore prayed to Him, in earnest, that he would have mercy on me.

"About this time I spent my spare time in retirement in the fields and woods, reading the New Testament and praying at different places.

"One morning as I was walking in front of the Tolbooth, thinking about my state, all on a sudden, a heavenliness came into my mind that I cannot describe,—men, women and children in the street, seemed all heavenly. For want of understanding this, I soon lost it.

"On the 10th of August, this year, we removed to the Castle at Edinburgh, where we were shut up with a large quantity of French prisoners, which made duty hard both night and day, till peace came to our relief. Here I had very few opportunities, even of hearing a sermon. We stopped here till March following. I have often wondered that I should still keep my serious impressions. In this month we received orders to march for Doncaster in Yorkshire. Our company went to Bawtry, where we stopped several weeks. Here I found a few Methodists, who held prayer meetings in a joiner's shop every Sunday night. I soon fell in amongst them, and received a new impulse for prayer. Soon after this we got dismissed and I returned home, and found a preacher labouring in this circuit of the name of Thomas Bartholomew. I found his preaching soon to open up the old wound, which drove me to earnest prayer, and the more I prayed the

ance and success until 1835, when, in consequence of the failure of his health, he removed to the Cape of Good Hope. He returned again to India for a short time, but was soon after-

---

worse I felt my state, till one Sunday I went with a few friends to a lovefeast at Shipley, when, just at the conclusion, my whole soul entered into the glorious liberty of the children of God. I came home singing the twelfth chapter of Isaiah. I could sing it for days and weeks, and scores of times since then. I soon found out that the way to heaven was the way of prayer, as well as in the use of all the other means of grace. I made a promise to the Lord, that by his gracious assistance, I would pray four times a day in private, twice a day in my family, and attend the house of God on the Sabbath as well as week-day preachings and prayer meetings, and class meeting at least once a week. I never recollect being stopped by the weather but once, though I lived most of my time in the country.

"I frequently feel humbled when I look back at so many privileges and such little improvement; but I feel gratitude when I look at so many kind interferences of a kind providence, and so many gracious manifestations of the love of Jesus Christ to my soul. But some say, 'what has it all done for me?' well, it has preserved me in a safe and happy way, from the year 1802 to the year 1854: and the best of all, at the last, it is not only good to live with, but better to die with."

For more than fifty years he was connected with the Sabbath school, discharging its various offices with great efficiency. * * * What he was as a leader is not easily told, but that he was possessed of talents for the suitable discharge of that duty seems early to have been discerned by those who were over him in the Lord. His piety, the soundness of his judgment, the singleness of his aim, his punctuality and

wards appointed to Western Australia. The voyage to this place proved a disastrous one, the vessel in which he and his family sailed became a perfect wreck, and for six weeks they were

readiness, the talent he possessed for comprehending the great varieties there are in a christian's experience, and giving in the most direct manner, suitable advice: these, with his power in prayer and scriptural knowledge, account in some measure for his success.

* * * * * * * *

In regard to his character in general and the estimation in which he was held, it may be safely stated, that, like Demetrius, he had "good report of all men and of the truth itself." He enjoyed the confidence of all; he was felt to be the property of all, and he well deserved to be held in such estimation. No one could doubt with what body of christians his sympathies were, or, whether Methodism stood high in his esteem; but he was as free from bigotry as he was from indifference; and these, without doubt, were some of the reasons that made him so valuable and acceptable as a visitor of the sick. This work may be said to have been almost his special business during the last fifteen or twenty years of his life. He went everywhere—he was welcome everywhere. * * But there is nothing that we can say that will delineate his manifold christian excellences. His praise was everywhere upon the lips of all wherever he was known; all thought of him as a friend, and in no instance was the esteem once given ever withdrawn; and such as he was, he was almost unconsciously. In his own eyes he was "the chief of sinners," and the "least of saints;" and it was his habitual acknowledgment, "by the Grace of God I am what I am." * * His decline, though gradual, was very perceptible. He was missed first from one well-known spot and then another—one friend's

exposed to the perils of the bush. A sketch of their adventures written by Mrs. Longbottom will prove interesting to many. She writes, "Having had no rest for several nights, at nine o'clock we went to bed. About one I was

house and then another—one customary occupation and then another; his feet forgot their accustomed ways, and even to the house of God, which was last abandoned, they went not. It was thus seen that he was journeying with certain steps to the "house appointed for all living." He seems to have realized the truth of some 'lines,' found, amongst others, in his Bible, and in his own hand-writing.

> "Now, Lord, in peace with thee and all below,
> Let me depart and to thy kingdom go.
> I have no doubt but I belong to thee,
> And shall be with thee to eternity.
> This from my heart believe, as thou art true,
> I am thy child—thy Son I know.
> I long to kiss that hand which oft me blest,
> Those feet that travelled to procure my rest,
> Those lips that me confest, and that blest head
> That bowed when all my sins were on it laid.
> Thy Cross my bed, my pillow then make soft;
> Thy ministers of flaming fire attend,
> And sing me sweetly to my journeys end!" AMEN.

His was a rare character, marked by a rare consistency, maintained for a lengthened term, and the memory of which will, without doubt, exercise a lasting influence. His end was a fitting sequel to his life.

E

roused by an unusual rolling of the vessel. Instantly I told my husband that I was sure we were in the surf. After a moment he was convinced that my fears were well founded; and, throwing on his rough jacket, was in the act of reaching his cap to go on deck, when the vessel struck. No time was now to be lost. Providentially we had all laid down in our clothes; I hurried on little William's shoes and cap, and, commending ourselves to God, we endeavoured to get on deck. We found the hatches down, and it was some time before we could make those on deck hear. When we did get out, an awful scene was before us. The sailors cut away the boat; but it drifted away the moment it was lowered. The captain had swum ashore with a rope; he lost his hold, and was unable to return. At length a sailor succeeded in reaching the shore with a rope, which he made fast, and then returned to render assistance to us. We put our dear boy over the side of the vessel first: the men handed him to the captain, who carried him through the surf. You may form some idea of what our feelings were when we knew that our only child was safe. It was now my turn; but I had not courage to jump overboard when the surf receded, and Mr. Longbottom was obliged to push me off. I lost my hold of the rope, and was several minutes under water. My dear William, seeing my situation, instantly plunged in after me, and laid hold of my dress. We were mercifully preserved, and all got safely through the dreadful surf, but I was extremely exhausted, and unable to stand when I reached the beach. All went behind a sand-bank, and lay down among the bushes to await the morning light. We were dreadfully cold, all being in our wet clothes, and unable to make a fire." After describing their interview with some natives, she speaks of the captain resolving upon finding an overland route to some station, and says,—"We had no alternative but either to accompany the ship's party, or be left behind in the bush. Accordingly, Mr. Longbottom prepared for our departure by packing up a pair of blankets, a few biscuits, and a little wine and water; the whole of which he fastened on his back, and we set out, 'not knowing whither we went.' But sleeping on the damp ground, together with struggling so long in the surf, had made me so stiff, and had brought on such rheumatism that I could scarcely walk at all. I dragged on about five miles, when I could go no farther. I believe God made the heart of the captain willing to return to our temporary tents which we had left standing; for he immediately consented to our proposal to go back. We arrived at the wreck about midnight, and found everything as we had left it." One of the boats was repaired, and a party found their way to a fishing station where they were kindly entertained. "The boat," says Mrs. Longbottom, "was leaky, the two sailors rowed, my husband steered, and I bailed out the water." They subsequently reached their station at Adelaide in safety. Mr. Longbottom laboured in various parts of Australia with great success until 1849, when his health failed again, and after a few months of feebleness and pain, he finished his course in the summer of that year.

In 1821 another individual destined to achieve for himself a good degree in the mission field, entered the society at Bingley, namely, the Rev. Thomas Cryer. He was a native of this place, and about the age of twenty-one was induced, chiefly through the influence of a pious sister, to give himself to the Lord. Seven years afterwards he entered the Wesleyan ministry, and, after labouring for a short time in this country, he sailed for Madras in 1829. For twenty-four years he devoted his talents and strength to the cause of God among the heathen. The Conference obituary is a most honourable testimony to his usefulness and worth. It says, "His zeal and vigour has seldom been surpassed. In spite of opposition before which an ordinary spirit would have quailed, in spite of the long delay of prosperity, which is the great and peculiar trial of the Eastern missionaries, in spite of the acute personal and family afflictions, his heart was undaunted and his faith unsubdued. Few of his fellow missionaries excelled him in power of utterance, in the adroitness and effect with which he exposed the sophisms of the Brahmin, in the hearty indignation of his invectives against the corruptions of heathenism, or in searching and persuasive appeals to the conscience." Few men in India ever laboured with more extensive success, or won such general esteem. Both natives and Europeans will be the crown of his rejoicing in the day of the Lord Jesus. It is to be regretted that no biography of this excellent missionary has been published. This partly may be accounted for by the fact that the Journals and papers which he carefully preserved, were so completely damaged by salt-water, owing to the vessel being wrecked in which his luggage was conveyed, as to become utterly useless. The loss of those documents was a source of intense regret to himself, as well as to many others. In 1852, Mr. Cryer removed from Bangalore to Madras, where he was appointed by the Conference. The day after his arrival he was seized with cholera, which soon reduced him to great feebleness. Immediately after the attack he said to Mrs. Cryer, "If I should be worse, don't be concerned about me; if I cannot speak, believe that all is right." To his medical attendant he said, "How happy to be able to trust in Jesus." After suffering three or four days, he finished his career of missionary heroism and toil by an end both peaceful and glorious. He left a widow and two children to mourn his loss. Thomas Cryer and William Longbottom were youthful companions in this town, where they are still remembered and revered. The Bingley society may feel honoured by giving to the mission work two such valuable men.

Some years afterwards this circuit supplied another useful labourer to the same sphere, namely, the Rev. Timothy Curtiss. He was a native of Wilsden, and entered the ministry in 1831. He was a man of eminent piety, and was much owned of God. He is spoken of as "grave, simple, and sincere," and was greatly beloved wherever he laboured. He was three and twenty years a missionary in the West Indies, where he died of cholera in 1854, in the 49th year of his age. Such men are worthy of all honour; such names ought not to be allowed to perish. If these pages do nothing more than help to keep their memorial before the church they will not have been written altogether in vain. Beside those already named this circuit has sent out another excellent and useful minister, namely, the Rev. James Clapham, who entered the ministry in 1836, and has laboured with great acceptance in the home work ever since; also, Messrs. Ainsworth and Brown, at present students in the Theological Institutions.

In the centenary year (1839), when the heart of Methodism was thrilled to its centre, when memories were awakened such as made the Methodist dead almost live again, when liberality burst forth in its largest and noblest forms, in this great movement the Bingley circuit took some humble part. The sum raised was nearly £300., one-third of which was contributed by the Townends of Cullingworth, under the names of fifteen different branches of that family. What an admonitory book is that centenary volume! In reading the list of contributors we are reminded how death and change have swept over thousands of families since that time. Bingley has not been exempt. Whilst the names of many that have passed away rise up and come over us with hallowed and mournful reflections, let us strive to realise the poet's words.

> " So live, that when thy summons comes,
> The innumerable caravan that moves
> To that mysterious realm, where each shall take
> His chamber in the silent halls of death,
> That thou, sustained and soothed, approach thy grave
> Like one who draws the drapery of his couch
> Around him, and lies down to pleasant dreams."

In 1839 died Mrs. Paulina Wyrill, a pious and devoted lady, daughter of the late Mr. John Sharp of this town. Mr. Sharp, her father, was not an ordinary man. His mechanical skill was considerable; his high christian character, his firmness of purpose combined with genuine kindness and benevolence of heart, secured the esteem of all who knew him. Mrs. Wyrill partook much of her father's qualities of heart and mind. She gave herself to the Lord in the prime of life. On her marriage she removed to Bradford, where she maintained her christian course during the brief period of domestic happiness which providence permitted her to enjoy. Her wedded life was transcient, for in one short year she became a wife and mother upon earth, and a glorified spirit in heaven. We name her case for the purpose of introducing the following interesting circumstance. Sometime before her death she purchased an Album, intended principally for contributions from ministers and eminent christians. She expressed a strong desire to have James Montgomery, Esq., the great christian poet, for her first contributor. The book was sent through the medium of friends, but on reaching the poet's residence, he had departed for the continent. Before his return the owner had passed into the spirit world. When Montgomery learned this fact he was much affected, and inscribed in the Album the following beautiful and original lines.

TO CONTRIBUTORS TO THIS ALBUM.

With fear and trembling on this volume look;
'Tis not a mortal's, but a spirit's book;
Wherein let none a line, a thought, indite,
That will not bear the day of judgment's light,
When every secret thing shall be made known,
By Him that sitteth on the "great white throne."

TO READERS OF THE CONTENTS.

With tender reverence on this volume look;
A saint in glory owns the humble book;
A bridal gift, by her consigned in trust;
To one dear friend when she returned to dust.
A link of love, unbroken, still to be
'Twixt him in time, her in eternity.

TO HER WHO LEFT THIS BOOK BEHIND.

Spirit made perfect! if sometimes thine ear,
Midst angels' songs, may earthly accents hear—

If, glancing from the unseen world on high,
Lines written on these pages meet thine eye—
Here, read, approve, while I presume to say
What thou, if prayer be made in heaven, dost pray!
" Our Father, God ! thy kingdom come ; thy will
" In earth as heaven, let all that breathe fulfil ,
" And, O ! since I am raised by sovereign grace,
" Thus in thy house to dwell and see thy face,
" May those below, with whom my heart was bound
" Be here with me in life eternal found."

The Mount, Sheffield,   JAMES MONTGOMERY.
Jan. 21st, 1840.

Methodism has kept its ground in this locality, and done its part along with other sections of the church, to elevate and bless the population around. To some our very name is an offence, and our good is evil spoken of; but all whose minds are free from prejudice, and who are capable of appreciating good intentions and good achievements, will admit that Methodism has been a great blessing to this town; and it is only such whose judgment we care for, and whose opinions are worth consideration. In the great and noble work of education, our people have taken a leading and active part. The zeal and liberality displayed in accomplishing this good work deserves to be placed upon permanent record. We more particularly refer to the Day School enterprize.

A Day School had existed for some time, which was conducted under the chapel. This place was found to be both unhealthy and inconvenient, and new premises were resolved upon, to include an Infant School-room and Master's residence. The friends of education were appealed to for assistance, which was followed by a prompt and liberal response, and the foundation stone was laid by Alfred Sharp, Esq., on the 28th of April, 1860.* The buildings are entirely of stone, in the early English style, from designs prepared by Mr. S. Jackson, architect, Bradford, on whom, as well as the builders, the whole reflects great credit. The

---

* A very interesting sight was presented on the occasion of the laying of the foundation stone. In the procession which passed through the town to witness the ceremony, the late Mrs. Dean and Thomas Longbottom rode together in a vehicle, and greatly enjoyed the scene. The former was 90 years of age and the latter upwards of 80. It was a happy thought to associate venerable age with youthful aspirations, and to recognize in both types of a past and present state of things.

large room is 54 feet by 30 feet, with two class rooms 22 feet by 15 feet. The Infant School room is 46 feet by 22 feet, with a class-room the same size as the others. The roof, which is open, is 35 feet high; and the whole is well ventilated, and warmed by hot water. The Master's house is a commodious and pleasant residence, and the entire structure is a credit to Methodism, and an ornament to the town. The opening ceremony took place on the 14th of August, 1861, on which occasion a large tea-meeting was held and addresses delivered by several ministers and friends. The total cost was £2799.1s.4d., namely, Ground, £406.3s.4d.; Buildings, £2334. 1s.; Sundries, £58. 16s. 3d. The amount raised was as follows—Subscriptions, £1186. 0s. 8d.: Ladies Bazaar, £213. 13s. 9d.; Collections in the Chapel, £343. 6s. 11d.; other contributions, £150; Grant from Wesleyan Training-school, £80.; Grant from Government, £826.; making the total receipts just to cover the expenses, which fact makes the effort still more praiseworthy.

The school is under the efficient care of Mr. T. J. Reynard, and the Infant department is conducted by Miss E. Beetham. The number

of scholars at present on the books is 352 in
the upper, and 160 in the infant school, making
a total of 512. The engraving which is given
as a frontispiece is an accurate representation
of the premises. The Sabbath school is in efficient
operation, and has a large number of
children in its charge, as the returns will show.
Methodism has not finished its work, nor had
its day in Bingley, any more than in other
places. Its efficiency for good has only yet been
partially developed. And when we speak of
Methodism we mean, "Christianity in earnest,"
as Dr. Chalmers called it. Only let those who
call themselves Wesleyan Methodists be what
their name imports, earnest, orderly, useful, and
consistent followers of Christ, and then the past
good which has been wrought through their
instrumentality will be but the shadow of what
is yet to follow. We court no favours, we fear
no enemies, we feel no chains, we lack no ordinances,
we envy not the success of other churches,
we make no pretentions to superiority in either
holiness or usefulness, but we do claim to be a
part of God's church, a wing of his army, a
branch of his great family. All that we want
as a people is a large effusion of the Divine

Spirit, and that effusion of the Spirit to result in a greater personal consecration of ourselves to the Lord, and a steady, consistent walk and conversation before the world. It is a question, a serious and important question, for the Wesleyans of Bingley to ask themselves whether a society numbering 360 members, 18 leaders, 6 local preachers, and 70 Sabbath school teachers is doing as much good as it ought to do? May the time soon come when this question can be answered in the affirmative.

We will now proceed to notice the other places in the circuit. The sketch of each is brief; but every item of interest has been taken hold of and placed before the reader in as condensed and intelligible a form as possible. No doubt the names of many excellent individuals might have been mentioned equally as deserving of notice as those alluded to. Want of space, however, is the principal cause of their omission. Anything approaching to invidious distinction we utterly disavow: it is not in the writer's heart, and he hopes it will not be found in his little book.

DENHOLME.

The name of this village is said to be of Anglo Saxon origin. From the year 1239 to the reign of Henry VIII, a great part of it belonged to Byland Abbey. At the dissolution of the monasteries in that reign it was granted to Sir Richard Tempest of Bolling hall. An extensive park once existed here which was noted for its numerous herds of fine red deer. It was broken up in the early part of the seventeenth century, when misfortune and change fell upon the Tempest family. Portions of the old park wall are still standing. The village is long and straggling, with an extensive population. Its atmosphere is cold, but bracing and healthy, and the inhabitants are a hardy and industrious class of people.

Methodism early found its way into this place. There is no tradition of Mr. Wesley having ever preached here, but there is no doubt that he several times passed through it on his way from Halifax to Keighley. A little incident occurred one day as he was riding along the village, a good woman living at Low Fold ran out of her house as he was passing, and begged to be permitted to shake hands with him. He was pleased with her earnestness and granted the request; and after giving her a few words of counsel, he put two shillings into her hand, and went on his way. How like the man! A small society was formed here sometime prior to 1760, but how long before cannot be ascertained. In that year we find it first appearing on the circuit book in the following terms, "Denholme, by William Grimshaw, 6s." Grimshaw preached here also, and seems to have brought this little flock beneath his fostering care. The class in 1763 consisted of seven members, five of which belonged to the Ogden family: the following are their names, Jeremiah Binns, Jonathan Hird, Michael Ogden, Grace Ogden, Mary Ogden, Edmund Ogden, Mary Ogden. The cause seems to have made but little progress during the next fourteen years, for in 1777 the number was only nine, namely, Abraham Binns, Susannah Brooksbank, Michael Ogden, Grace Ogden, Abigal Ackroyd, Robert Bartle, John Baxandale, Hannah Midgley, Elizabeth Barge. The Ogden family were the principal supporters of Methodism for many years. Michael lived in the Low Fold, and for a considerable time the preaching was held in his house. A gravestone in front of the chapel records his death in 1797, aged 75, and also that of his wife, Grace Ogden, in 1803, aged 85. A tablet placed inside of the chapel, at the west end, announces the death of Edmund Ogden in 1822, aged 73, along with several of his children; and also, Martha, his widow, who died in 1846, aged 91. Betty Bartle, who is now living and in her 94th year, has long been a member of society in Denholme; she came to live with the Ogdens when she was only ten years of age, and speaks of them as steady, zealous upholders of the little church in the day when it was but small and feeble. In 1793 the first place of worship was erected, which consisted of an upper room, with two cottages underneath. The ground on which it was built was formerly a plantation, and a place of great resort for cock-fighting and other brutal games on the sabbath, for which Denholme was once notorious. This small chapel sufficed for all their wants until 1823, when a considerable enlargement was made, and, with the exception of the organ loft and vestry, is the same as it is found at present. The expenses incurred by this enlargement entailed a heavy debt upon the trustees, but a special providence raised them up a friend in the person of Mr. Jonas Foster, who most generously made provision in his will for the payment of all the debt. A tablet in the chapel thus records this act of liberality,

"SACRED TO THE MEMORY OF"

"JONAS FOSTER, OF DENHOLME, GROCER,"

Who departed this life the 23rd of December, 1826, aged 56.

"He was for many years the managing trustee of this chapel, and, when it was encumbered, he advanced out of his own private money toward paying the debt so incurred, and without requiring from his co-trustees any security, upwards of £400., which in a codicil to his will is directed not to be claimed by his executors. He has also in the same codicil acquitted the trustees of the Sunday school from a loan of £50. These acts of benevolent charity are deservedly recorded to his memory."

Beside these instances of liberality, Mr. Foster in other ways manifested his generosity, especially towards the local preachers of the circuit. Seven or eight years after the enlargement, the vestry and organ loft were built and the organ purchased, which occasioned the present debt, and in 1838 the Sabbath school was erected. In 1861 the Denholme society supplied two useful young men as candidates for the Wesleyan ministry, namely, Messrs. William Ainsworth and Joseph Brown.

A remarkable circumstance in the life of Jonathan Saville took place in this village, a condensed account of which we will lay before the reader. The house which was the scene of these events has been pulled down. It formerly stood near the high road on the left hand side, a few hundred yards from the toll-gate on Manuels height, going towards Denholme.

Jonathan Saville, a well-known local preacher, occasionally visited this circuit. He was called "little Jonathan" on account of the smallness of his stature. His early life was marked by great poverty and cruel treatment. He was born at Great Horton, and when a child was sent to the workhouse, and afterwards apprenticed to a person at Denholme to learn to spin. His master, contrary to engagement, sent him to work in the coal pit, where he endured great hardships. "One day," he says, "when I was about ten years of age, I was sitting upon a low stool in the passage of the house, spinning. It was a very cold day, and I went to the fire to warm myself. One of my master's daughters came and pushed me roughly away, I fell with my thigh under me, and it was broken. I crawled into a room and lay down on the bed. When my master came home they told him, 'Jonathan has turned sulky, and has gone and laid him down in bed.' He came to me and said if I did not get up and spin he would knock my brains out. I tumbled off the bed as well as I could, and supported myself by a chair, my thigh bent under me, and I fell to the ground. He dragged me down upon the low stool, and made me spin for the rest of the day. No doctor was called to set my thigh, nor did any of the women show me any compassion. My moanings were laughed at. I used to go to sleep at night holding the bone in its place as well as I could. In this condition I remained between two and three years." He then describes his removal back again to the workhouse. "My master set out with me on his back, my broken leg dangling like a dead hare. We overtook a lad to whom my master offered sixpence to carry me as far as Queenshead. There I was put into a cart which was going down to Horton, the shaking of the cart made me scream for agony." What a picture of human sufferings! He subsequently recovered the use of his leg, but owing to his cruel treatment his growth was stunted, and his body deformed. He found religion, and the grace of God made him a marvellous instrument of good to thousands. He became very popular, and was often called upon to preach on special occasions. We mention him in this place chiefly to relate what follows. Some years after he became a preacher, he was invited to preach at Denholme on behalf of Missions, and whilst there he was requested to visit a sick woman. "When I got into the house," he says, "I was taken with a fit of musing. The woman seeing me said, 'Did you once live here?' I gave a look back and inwardly exclaimed, 'What has God done for poor me!' And then I thought of my three or four years of suffering in that very house, for there it was that my thigh was broken, and I said, 'Is it possible that the Lord should have brought me to pray with that woman. O Lord, now thou hast repaid me for all my sufferings.'" Jonathan Saville died in 1842, aged 83 years.

CULLINGWORTH.

Cullingworth, like many other places in the West Riding of Yorkshire, has greatly increased in size and population. Within the recollection of many living persons it has risen from a small and insignificant hamlet to a thriving and prosperous village. The large manufacturing establishment of Messrs. Townend has drawn together hundreds of industrious operatives, whose minds and morals have been cared for by the erection of schools and places of worship belonging to various denominations.

Although Methodism entered this place a little later than some others, it has, nevertheless, taken a prominent and influential position in the circuit. It is said that Mr. Grimshaw occasionally preached here, which is not at all improbable, but nothing reliable can be ascertained respecting his visits; neither can it be found out at what precise time or under what circumstances the Methodist society was first formed. As early as 1777 we find a class existing including eight members, namely, Jeremiah Binns, Amy Binns, Joseph Waddington, Sarah Waddington, Jeremiah Rhodes, Barbara Hallendrake, Jonas Hallendrake, Joseph Crowther. It is presumed that this was the first class, and that its formation took place about the above-named year, inasmuch as there is no mention made of Cullingworth in the circuit book until that time. There is no return made in 1778, but in 1779 we find Jeremiah Rhodes down as the leader, with the following members: Jeremiah Rhodes, Joseph Rhodes, Joseph Waddington, Sarah Waddington, Barbara Hollingdrake, Henry Mitchell, Tomison Waddington, Mary Hollingdrake, Joseph Crowder, Mary Crowder, Timothy Rhodes, Hannah Jowet, Thomas Dixon, Judith Dixon, Roger Robertshaw. Jeremiah Rhodes held the office of leader for nearly forty years. Mr. William Ellison, who is now the oldest member of society in Cullingworth, when a youth, met in his class, and speaks of him as a steady, consistent, and useful man of God. Another class existed in 1795 of which Timothy Rhodes was the leader, and continued until 1801, when it was merged into the one led by Jeremiah. Some time after the death of the last named person, David Binns became the leader. David, it is said, was somewhat peculiar in his views. About the time he held this office an innovation was made on the old fashion of wearing small clothes, by the adoption of trousers. He looked upon the new mode of dress as a sad developement of pride, and for christian professors to adopt it he deemed a most reprehensible exhibition of inconsistency. David was not alone in these views. The writer has often been amused when hearing elderly people describe the struggles of that transition period. It has been said that David carried his views so far as to object to any one meeting in his class that refused to conform to the old style of garment. The latter statement is probably an exaggeration.

The first-place in which the Methodists conducted divine worship was the house of Joseph Waddington, and afterwards that of John Northrop. These were two staunch old members of the little church, and their wives were truly mothers in Israel. In the early part of the present century they found themselves straightened for want of room, and some began to talk about getting a chapel, but their number being so small, and the prospect of being able to raise the means not encouraging, they hardly knew how to proceed. In these difficult circumstances, the zeal of a godly woman came to their help, and proved the means of accomplishing their wishes. Mary, or, as she was better known by, Mally Northrop, wife of the above-mentioned John Northrop, told her husband one day that she had been thinking about an old barn, which stood near their house, what an excellent place it would be for a chapel, and that she had been strongly impressed to go to the owner and request him to give it for that purpose. The property belonged to a person named John Ellison, one of the most unlikely individuals to grant such a favour. With true womanly perseverance Mally pressed her application, and so far succeeded as to get him to request a day's consideration, at the expiration of which time, to the surprise of many, he consented to give both the land and the materials of the old building, on condition of having a front pew in the gallery secured for his use for ever; which, of course, was readily granted. After this steps were taken to raise the funds necessary to erect the chapel, and we may form some idea of the size of the place from an expression of the Rev. Isaac Muff, one of the circuit ministers, when informed of the movement, he said, "I cannot see where your congregation is to come from, except they come out of the clouds." The building was completed and opened for divine worship in 1806. The society went on for some years without anything transpiring worth naming until about 1817, when a most remarkable and extensive revival took place. For some time before this the state of things was at the lowest point, a few mourned over the dead and desolate condition of the church, when one night after a prayer-meeting it was proposed that they all should fall upon their knees, and in penitent and humble prayer seek the out-pouring of the Holy Ghost. They did so, and an overwhelming influence came down upon them. From this meeting the quickening energy spread through the village, scores were brought to God, rejoicing or inquiring penitents were to be found in almost every house; "So mightily grew the word of God and prevailed." At the above-named meeting were present Joseph Northrop and the late Mrs. Midgley, who were the first penitents in the revival. The former is still pursuing his way to heaven; the latter, after a life of christian consistency fell asleep in Jesus. Mrs. Midgley is spoken of as a most excellent and devoted woman, and one who adorned the doctrine of God her Saviour in all things. In this revival was converted the late Robert Townend, Esq., of Broughton near Manchester, who, by his life and devotedness to God's cause, lived to prove the genuineness of the work which then was wrought. Some years after this Mr. George Townend was brought to God, and became a zealous leader and a hearty friend to the cause of Methodism. He died at Cullingworth, and his name is still held in affectionate remembrance. Mr. Thomas Anderton was another greatly esteemed member. He was a deeply pious young man, and one who walked humbly with his God. His death, which was awfully sudden, produced a solemn impression in the village. Thomas Robertshaw also left a name which is hallowed in the memories of many. Having experienced this enlargement in numbers the old chapel was found to be much too small, and a new one became the subject of conversation. Help was forthcoming, and in 1825 a new sanctuary reared its head, which was opened on Friday the 10th, Sunday the 12th, and Monday the 13th of June in that year. The ministers who officiated on the occasion

were the Rev. T. Lessey, the Rev. R. Wood, the
Rev. David Stoner, and Mr. Wm. Dawson. The
crowd on the Sabbath was so great that they
had to be divided into three congregations, one
in the new chapel, another in the old one, and
one out of doors, all held at the same time.
The amount raised by public collections amounted to £243. 0s. 4¼d., in addition to £400. from
private subscriptions, making a total of £643.,
which in that day was a noble sum to raise.

The year after this chapel was opened,
Cullingworth, which had previously been in the
Keighley circuit was joined to Bingley, as was
also Denholme at the same time. Methodism
in this village has kept on its way during the
years that have followed, subject to those fluc-
tuations which are incident to all churches, but
still always preserving the great principles of
vital godliness in its midst. In 1861 another
noble enterprise was achieved by the enlargement of the chapel, and the purchase of an organ
at an outlay of £1087., the whole of which was
realised. The Wesleyans of Cullingworth have
now a place of worship, which, for neatness and
convenience is exceeded by very few village
chapels in the kingdom. A Wesleyan Day

School is also in efficient operation, under the care of Mr. Thomas Howe, master. The building, which is in the Gothic style, was opened in 1851. The school numbers upwards of two hundred scholars.

WILSDEN.

Methodism in this village has undergone various changes. As stated in the former pages of this work, some of the first Methodist preachers visited and formed a society at Ling Bob at a very early period, which continued for some time, but afterwards went under the name of Wilsden Hill. These members were no doubt some of the fruits of those labours which William Darney celebrated in his long hymn when he sung,

"And at Ling Bob sometimes at noon,
The Gospel Trump we sound."

The first class was established a considerable time before 1760, probably in 1747, when Thos. Lee preached there, which he called "Lingbobin." In 1760 Ling Bob appears upon the books for the first time. The earliest item for quarterage is, "October 16, 1760, Ling Bob, by Wm. Grimshaw, 10s." There are no more payments until nearly two years afterwards, but there is no doubt the money was sent along with some other place. The next entry is, "Jan. 14, 1762, Ling Bob, 5s.: Thornton, 7s. 3d., by W. Grimshaw." "Ling Bob and Haworth, 11s. by ditto." "Oct. 14, 1762, Wilsden Hill, by Jeremiah Robertshaw, 8s. 10d." "April 14, 1763, Oakes and Wilsden Hill, 13s. 6d." Oakes is supposed to have been a place near Allerton. This little society kept fluctuating, and its waning light grew less and less, until 1787, in which year the quarterage had fallen down to 3s., when it utterly disappeared. The following are the names of the members of society in 1763: Robt. Fowler, weaver, leader; Caleb Jennings, weaver; Alice Hill, yeoman; John Soller, weaver; Judith Wilkinson; John Smith, blacksmith; "dead" written against the last name: William Wilkinson, weaver; Hannah Bentley, spinner; Martha Patterson, ditto: Hannah Firth, ditto; Sarah Priestley, ditto; Susannah Patterson, ditto; Joseph Pickles of Thornton, weaver; Mary Watters, cordwainer; Thomas Dobinson, Mary Dobinson, Elizabeth Jackson, Jonas Bower,

Hannah Wood, Judith Forth, Martha Wilkinson, another Martha Wilkinson, Sus. Woolmern, Mary Firth, Sarah Bankroft, Jon. Bentley, in all twenty-six.

Caleb Jennings, the second on the list, was great grandfather to Mr. Thomas Leach of Wilsden. He seems to have left the neighbourhood and gone to reside in the Bradford circuit, for we find him mentioned in Stamps' History of Methodism as a leader in 1781, namely, "Coat Gap; sixteen members, Caleb Jennings, leader." In 1777, John Soller becomes the leader of the Wilsden Hill class, until 1779, when he removes and Alice Hill takes his place. In 1781 there stands written against her name, "dead, wants a leader."

A long silence rests upon the cause of Methodism in this place for a quarter of a century nearly, after the year 1787, when the society became extinct. In 1807 we find it making its first efforts to return. Richard Nixon of Harden, a zealous local preacher, was one of the first to regain a footing by obtaining a house to preach in. This house was occupied by Matthew Patchett, and worship was conducted in it for some time afterwards. A class was formed consisting of two members, namely, Matthew Patchett and Seth Wright. In addition to the smallness of their number they laboured under another inconvenience in carrying on their little meetings, one of them could sing but was unable to read, the other however could read but possessed no vocal powers; so one gave out the hymn and the other sang, and between them they managed to hold on their way until others joined them. In 1810 the Rev. Robt. Jackson, then stationed in Bingley, visited them and began to hold regular services, assisted by R. Nixon, Samuel Atkinson, and other local preachers. After remaining in the above-named place for some time, the preaching was removed to a house on Old Dame's Green, in the occupation of Hannah Jowett, who kept a dame's school, which fact no doubt gave the name to the locality. This old lady was a member of society, and lived to a great age. Nearly all the female children of the village for two or three generations passed through her hands. She unfortunately met with a melancholy end. Being left alone, she knelt down to pray near the fire, which caught her garments, and was so severely burnt that she expired soon afterwards, in the 93rd year of her age. This occurred in 1826. Sometime before this took place the meetings were removed from her house to James Firth's of Wilsden Hill, and continued to be held there until the first chapel was built in 1823. The erection of this chapel was accomplished amidst great opposition, the circumstances of which had better remain in oblivion. The opening sermons were preached by the Rev. Messrs. J. Mann, A. E. Farrar, and David Stoner. A Sunday school was soon after established, from which several persons have risen to honour and usefulness in the christian ministry, such as the Rev. Timothy Curtiss, the Rev. James Clapham, the Rev. Ingham Sutcliffe of the British American Conference. The society continued to prosper, and in 1847 a new chapel was resolved upon, the foundation stone of which was laid on Shrove-Tuesday of that year, by Mr. Matthew Patchett, the oldest member in Wilsden. The building was completed and opened in the following October, and sermons were preached on the occasion by the Reverend Messrs. Beaumont, Everett, Booth, Savage, and Mr. Wm. Dawson. It is a neat, well built place of worship, and when the re-painting which it is now undergoing is completed, will be a beautiful and commodious sanctuary. It contains upwards of five hundred sittings, a portion of which are free. A Wesleyan Day School was opened on Shrove-Tuesday, 1857, by the Rev. W. M. Punshon, which now numbers about 200 children, under the direction of Mr. Rymer, master.

Methodism in Wilsden has proved a great blessing, and, along with other denominations, has helped to scatter the ignorance and superstition which once rested on the village. If Ling Bob was honoured by having the gospel trumpet sounded there by such men as Maskew and Lee, and Mitchell, and Darney, it has also been rendered notorious by giving a name to a celebrated fortune teller called the Ling Bob Witch. The woman who bore this name was Hannah Green, she practiced her art for forty years, and died at Yeadon in 1810, after saving upwards of £1000. Witchcraft and witches cannot stand before the advancing intelligence of the age. Sunday schools, Day schools and places of worship everywhere are all engaged in one determined crusade against ignorance and superstition in every form. Few villages in this neighbourhood are more highly favoured in their religious and educational privileges than this place. The Church of England, Independents, Primitives and Wesleyans have each a place of worship, and a Sabbath school; beside these there are three Day Schools, and a Mechanics Institute, the latter having one of the best village libraries in the kingdom.

HARDEN.

Harden was amongst the first places in this neighbourhood where Methodism set up its banner. As early as 1747 we find Thomas Lee accepted an invitation to preach there, as well as at Thornton and other places in that locality. He says in his autobiography, "Many found peace with God, and a society was raised in each place." The members at the first met in Bingley, but in 1763 we find them existing as a class with Abraham Binns of Harden Brow for their leader. Sometime about 1770, Harden became a distinct society, with its numbers separately reported, but still continued to pay its quarterage along with Bingley. The names of those who were members a hundred years ago may be seen by referring to pages 22 and

23. The following are those returned in 1777: Christopher Townend, John Wade, John Jackson, John Bower, Samuel Brashaw, Ann Brashaw, William Hargreaves, John Sugden, Thomas Dixon, Ann Binns, Timothy Rhodes, Jonas Bailey, James Brier, Abraham Wilkinson, Mary Wilkinson, William Waterhouse, Abraham Binns, Isabella Binns, Isaac Wilkinson, Robert Hill, Abraham Hill, Sarah Garnett, George Wildman, total twenty-four. In 1782 the numbers fell down to seventeen, but ten years afterwards we find them up to fifty-one. There are several individuals mentioned in the above list about whom we wish to offer some remarks. John Jackson was great grandfather to Mr. E. Laycock, local preacher, Bingley. Mr. Jackson was a noted Methodist in Harden; his religion was sound and practical, and for godliness and honesty he had a good report of all men. He lived near the Grange, now called St. Ives, in a pleasant situation close by the gardens of Mr. Ferrand. The road from Bingley being a beautiful and romantic walk, it was customary for numbers of Methodist friends from this town to take provisions with them, and spend agreeable visits at his house, invariably closing their

christian intercourse with a lively prayer meeting. He had two brothers, Samson and Joseph, both pious men and members of the Methodist society. A somewhat singular circumstance is preserved in the family to the following effect. When Sampson fell sick unto death, John was sent for in all haste to see him. On his way he was startled by hearing strange and unearthly music, of such unutterable sweetness as to be beyond all description. Not being of a superstitious or visionary turn of mind, he concluded that it came from some house or place of worship down in the valley at Bingley; he listened but could perceive no sound coming from thence. On reaching his brother's residence he found he had died a short time before he arrived. His strong belief was that the music he heard was the song of the angels bearing his departed brother to his heavenly rest. Whilst we hesitate to believe in the supernatural character of this circumstance, we must bear in mind that "there are more things in heaven and earth than our philosophy has ever dreamt of." The William Hargreaves who appears amongst the number, was the same individual about whom another singular event is recorded—*see page* 51. William Waterhouse of Hill End,* another member of the class, lived until he was 95 years of age, and his mother, who resided with him, reached 103. This old lady was truly an *old* Methodist. We find her name down in the Wilsden Hill class for 1777,

---

* The place where Mr. Waterhouse lived was a part of what was once a large and respectable mansion. In the middle of the seventeenth century Samuel Sunderland, Esq., a retired merchant from London resided here. A notorious and daring burglary once occurred on these premises, the particulars of which will be found in the following account taken from the "Civil and Miscellaneous History of the District within ten miles of Leeds." Harden Hall is mentioned in the extract as the scene of this robbery, but tradition is unanimous in placing it at Hill End or Hill House.

"Samuel Sunderland, Esq., who flourished in the reign of Charles I. and in the Commonwealth, resided at Harden Hall, not far from Bingley. He was one of the richest men of his age, and had accumulated an enormous quantity of gold coin which he preserved in bags placed on two shelves in a private part of his house. Two individuals who resided at Collingham, and who were in circumstances above want, though not above temptation, determined to rob Mr. Sunderland of the whole, or at any rate of a considerable quantity of his gold; and in order to prevent the chance of successful pursuit, they persuaded a blacksmith at Collingham to put shoes on their horses' feet backwards way. They arrived at Harden Hall, and, according to their purpose, took away as much gold in bags as they thought they could carry off, and notwithstanding the communication of an alarm to the family before they left the house, they succeeded

from which place she appears to have removed to keep the house of her son, An old resident of Harden who lived next door to her, describes her as a "plump, round, healthy looking little body," and mentions an amusing circumstance of a person mistaking her for the wife of her

---

in accomplishing their retreat. The weight of the gold they took away was too much for their jaded horses, and they were compelled to leave part of it on Black Moor, where it was afterwards found by some persons of Chapeltown, whose descendants are still living at that village at the present day. It so happened that the robbers had taken a dog with them on their expedition, and this animal, in the hurry of their retreat, they left behind them fastened up in the place from which they had taken the gold. The friends and neighbours of Mr. Sunderland, who had determined upon pursuit, immediately saw in this dog the means of detecting the offenders. Having broken one of its legs to prevent it running too fast for their horses they turned it loose. It proceeded, notwithstanding its excruciating pain, to Collingham, and went directly to the house of its owners. The pursuers arrived, burst open the door, and found the thieves in the very act of counting the money. They were sent to York, tried, and condemned to die; and their own apprentice was compelled to act the part of their executioner. The young man, though innocent of any capital participation in the robbery, was so horror-struck by the deed he had been compelled to perform, that he criminated himself and followed the fate of his masters."

A publican was mixed up with the affair, which occasioned the saying, "Like the landlord of Collingham, you'll come in for your share."

son, and expressing surprise that he should marry a woman so much younger than himself. A tombstone in Bingley churchyard bears the following: "Mary Waterhouse, widow, died March 5, 1822, aged ONE HUNDRED AND THREE.

> "Her house she made a house of prayer,
> She wrestled with her God,
> She prayed for all her family,
> She wished to do them good."

Divine service was conducted for many years in private houses, principally at Samuel Brashaw's, next to the bridge and opposite to the blacksmith's shop; also at the houses of Joseph Barraclough, miller, near Harden Beck, and Wm. Leach, in Harden Lane. After these, a room over a stable in Harden Lane was occupied, and occasionally preaching was held at Hill End. In 1813 steps were taken to build a chapel, and amongst those who took an active part in the effort were the members of the family of Mrs. Hannah Sharp. Her sons John, James and William were amongst the first trustees, and the latter, with two daughters, has found his last resting place in the grave yard adjoining the chapel. Mrs. Sharp was a consistent member of society, and generously entertained the preachers for a number of years. Amongst the prominent and active Methodists of that day was Lot Brashaw, a leader. After a long course of usefulness, he unhappily became separated from the society, owing to some evidence he gave upon a trial which brought upon him the displeasure of the village. Jonas Howgate was another zealous leader whose name is still held in pious remembrance. Two well known local preachers also resided here, namely, Henry Bailey and Richard Nixon: the former was better known as the "charcoal burner." The work went on and prospered, and more room being required, an enlargement of the chapel was made in 1835. Nothing of any interest occurred until the late Reform agitation burst like a tempest on the connexion. Harden, small as it was, was terribly shaken by the storm. The writer has no wish to go into the details of that movement. Some of the persons who stood in the van of both parties are now sleeping together in their graves; and, it is hoped that those who survive have long ceased to cherish hostile feelings towards each other. The possession of the chapel was the point aimed at by both sides. The case was tried before the Court of Chancery in London, and terminated in favour of the Connexional trustees. Through the persevering efforts of the Rev. Samuel Merrill, the superintendent minister at that time, assistance was obtained from various quarters, and the trustees came out of the fiery ordeal with their possession legally secured, all the expenses incurred by the trial met, and with no more debt upon the premises than before the struggle commenced. One of those who took an active part in the business was Mr. Robert Colton, the oldest surviving member of society in Harden. His heart is still warm in its attachments to Methodism, in connection with which he has spent upwards of half a century. It is somewhat amusing to hear him relate the adventures of those stormy times. A brief allusion to the subject is sufficient to rouse him like some old veteran soldier, "who shoulders his crutch, and fights his battles o'er again."

ELDWICK, &c.

The Eldwick society was formed about 1766, but prior to that date the members residing there were connected with Bingley. The East Morton society in 1795 numbered 28 members, with John Watson for their leader, and West Morton 5 members and Isaac Wilkinson for their leader. Preaching has been conducted at Gilstead and Crossflatts for a great number of years, and also at Micklethwaite for some time; the classes at these three places form a part of the Bingley society.

We have now completed the task we took in hand, but not without a strong sense of the imperfect manner in which it has been performed. Whilst it has been a work of some little toil, it has also been one of spiritual profit to the writer's own soul. Whilst inquiring into the circumstances amidst which Methodism has arisen and progressed, and whilst contemplating the devoted and blessed men and women who were its members and supporters in bygone times, he has felt a quickening influence come over him, producing an earnest prayer that their spirit of love and mantle of zeal might fall upon their successors. The Methodist dead have a living voice, and one object of the writer has been to convey that voice into the ears and hearts of those who at present fill the places of their departed fathers. Methodism in the Bingley circuit never occupied larger ground, or stood upon a firmer basis, and never had more numerous and attentive congregations; but, like all other churches, more or less, we want more self-sacrificing, more divine enthusiasm and personal devotedness to our one great Master and Lord; not rant, not noise, not a wild unmeaning zeal, but a simple earnestness, which, whilst it will not run into fanaticism on the one side, will not suffer the pious ardour of the soul to be smothered and quenched by the forms and conventionalities of religion on the other. The writer before he closes, wishes to say that whilst he has used the terms Methodist and Methodism frequently in the preceding pages, it has not been in the spirit of bigotry, not to glorify Methodism, but the God of Methodism. A hundred years possession, however, of the ground arduously and honourably won, entitles us to lift our flag, not of sectarian defiance, but of religious independence. Before Almighty God, the great searcher of hearts, we are all unprofitable servants; but amongst surrounding churches we ask not for, neither do

we acknowledge, either in liberty of conscience or freedom of worship, any second place. As a people all that we want is a right to serve God, and room to do good. At the mast head of our good old ship there still floats bravely the storm blown banner of a hundred years, and upon it are yet inscribed those well known words:
"THE FRIENDS OF ALL, THE ENEMIES OF NONE."

A LIST OF MINISTERS WHO HAVE LABOURED IN BINGLEY.

WHEN IN THE HAWORTH CIRCUIT.

1753 Jonathan Maskew, John Whitford, Enoch Williams, Joseph Jones, William Shent, John Edwards.
1755 William Grimshaw, John Nelson, John Scholefield.
1758 James Oddie, Alexander Coates.
1765 Isaac Brown, John Atley, Nicholas Manners, James Stephens, R. Costerdine.
1766 J. Brown, J. Shaw, R. Costerdine, J. Atley.
1767 R. Costerdine, Joseph Guildford, J. Whittam, Thomas Cherry.
1768 Thos. Mitchell, J. Guildford, W. Ellis, T. Newall.
1769 T. Mitchell, G. Hudson, Thos. Wride, D. Evans.
1770 R. Seed, G. Hudson, D. Evans.
1771 Jeremiah Robertshaw, Stephen Proctor, John Poole.
1772 Thomas Johnson, John Poole, Thos. Tatton.
1773 T. Johnson, E. Slater, R. Costerdine,

1774 R. Costerdine, R. Seed, R. Swann.
1775 Thos. Taylor, R. Swann, Samuel Bardsley.

WHEN IN THE KEIGHLEY CIRCUIT.

1776 Thomas Taylor, Samuel Smith.
1777 John Allen, William Brammah.
1778 J. Allen, G. Hudson.
1779 James Hindmarsh, G. Hudson.
1780 Samuel Bradburn, W. Simpson.
1781 Isaac Brown, R. Hayward.
1782 Ditto William Hunter.
1783 B. Rhodes, Thos. Mitchell.
1784 Parson Greenwood, John Booth.
1785 Ditto Joseph Entwisle.
1786 Joseph Bradford, John Beanland.
1787 William Blagborne, Thos. Dixon, Thos. Shaw.
1788 John Wood, T. Bartholomew, William Blagborne, R. Hayward, super.
1789 John Wood, John Peacock, J. Beanland.
1790 J. Booth, J. Grant.
1791 Do. J. Ridall.
1792 George Storey, Duncan Kay.
1793 R. Hopkins, W. Hainsworth.
1794 Ditto W. Stephenson.
1795 E. Jackson, T. Tattershall.
1796 Ditto John Leach.
1797 John Moon, S. Gates.
1798 Ditto Ditto
1799 T. Crowther, R. Dall.
1800 Ditto M. Martindale.
1801 M. Martindale, J. Denton.
1802 T. Bartholomew, ditto

1803 T. Bartholomew, J. Crowther.
1804 J. Crowther, G. Gibbon.
1805 J. Crosby, G. Gibbon, I. Muff,
1806 Ditto I. Muff, J. Collier,
1807 J. Stamp, J. Collier, J. Newton,

BINGLEY CIRCUIT.

1808 J. Needham, W. Scholefield.
1809 Ditto R. Jackson.
1810 Alexander Suter, R. Jackson.
1811 Ditto Joseph Boddycoat.
1812 T. Rogerson, W. Rennison.
1813 W. Ratcliffe, W. Lord.
1814 Ditto ditto
1815 H. Taft, G. Mainwaring.
1816 Ditto ditto
1817 J. Sedgwick, J. E. Beaumont.
1818 J. Blackett, ditto
1819 C. Gloyne, J. Armitage.
1820 Thomas Stanley.
1821 Ditto
1822 John Farrar, sen.
1823 Ditto
1824 John Sumner.
1825 F. Derry
1826 Samuel Sugden, W. O. Booth.
1827 Ditto ditto
1828 C. Ratcliffe, J. Nicholson, J. W. Etheridge.
1829 Ditto J. Nicholson, B. Slack, S. Wilson, supernumerary.
1830 P. Garrett, J. Garrett.
1831 Ditto ditto

AND THE NEIGHBOURHOOD. 113

1832	P. Garrett,	John Haigh.	
1833	T. Hamer,	ditto	
1834	Ditto	ditto	
1835	Ditto	T. Eckersley.	
1836	Peter Prescott,	ditto	
1837	Ditto	John Lewis..	
1838	John Lewis,	A. Freeman.	
1839	Ditto	ditto	
1840	E. Batty,	J. Callaway.	
1841	Ditto	W. Jessop.	
1842	T. Garbutt, 1st.	W. Jessop.	
1843	Ditto	ditto	
1844	W. Level,	W. Winterburn,	W. M'Kitrick, super.
1845	Ditto	ditto	ditto
1846	B. Frankland,	ditto	ditto
1847	Ditto	B. Pearce.	
1848	Ditto	Samuel Allen.	
1849	Samuel Allen,	G. Greenwood.	
1850	James Catton,	ditto	
1851	Ditto	ditto	
1852	S. Merrill,	A. Learoyd.	
1853	Ditto	W. Wilson 4th.	
1854	Ditto	ditto	
1855	I. Dennison,	C. G. Turton.	
1856	S. Timms,	ditto	
1857	Ditto	ditto	
1858	Ditto	J. B. Dawson.	
1859	J. D. Julian,	ditto	
1860	Ditto	ditto	
1861	Ditto	Henry Cattle.	
1862	Samuel Taylor,	John Ward.	

H

SABBATH SCHOOLS IN THE CIRCUIT.

The following schedule represents the Sabbath school interest in connexion with the Wesleyan Methodists in this circuit. And as so many feel interested in these institutions, having been in their younger days scholars or teachers, or are at present engaged therein, these statistics will, no doubt, prove acceptable; and more particularly so at the present time when a Circuit Sabbath School Union is about being formed.

	SCHOLARS.	TEACHERS.
Bingley	415	70
Cullingworth	287	72
Denholme	164	63
Harden	100	18
Wilsden	239	42
Morton	94	30
Eldwick Beck and Cragg	62	15
Micklethwaite	54	9
Gilstead	69	17
TOTALS	1484	336

These schools are conducted at an aggregate outlay of £130. per annum, including rents, books, rewards, and festival expenses.

CHAPELS IN THE CIRCUIT.

The following table will show when each chapel was built or enlarged.

	DATE OF ERECTION.			ENLARGED.	
Bingley	1770	179—	1816		
Cullingworth		1806	1825	1861	
Denholme			1793	1823	
Harden			1813	1835	
Wilsden		1823	1847		
Morton		1828	1846		
Micklethwaite			1853		
Eldwick Cragg			1815		
Eldwick Beck			1832		

The total debt upon the chapel property of the circuit amounts to upwards of £3000. A united effort to reduce this sum, and employ the money saved in interest in supporting a third minister on the ground, is what is greatly needed, and must one day be taken in hand, if Methodism is to fully accomplish its mission in this locality.

JOHN HARRISON AND SON, PRINTERS, BINGLEY.

ADDENDA.

Considerable search was made to find some reference to Mr. Grimshaw's visits to Bingley, but without success, when, just before the last of these pages were struck off by the printer, the following passage in the life of the celebrated Richard Burdsall was met with. Being at Eldwick on a visit he was invited to hear Mr. Grimshaw at Bingley the next day. He says "At this invitation my heart glowed within me, and burned with desire until the time came. The next day happened to be new year's day, new style, and a very stormy, snowy day it proved. When we got to the place, I trembled so much with the cold, that I thought it would be impossible for me to bear it long. The place of worship was a barn, which had been fitted up for the purpose with deal seats and pulpit. The very appearance of the congregation was pleasing to me. After waiting for a short time, a broad set, sharp-looking little man appeared habited as a layman, and buttoned up from the storm. Having quickly loosed his garments, in a moment he was in the pulpit, and giving out a hymn, the people sung like thunder. His voice in prayer seemed to me as it had been the voice of an angel. After prayer he took a little bible out of his pocket and read the following words for his text: *Glory to God in the highest, on earth peace, good will toward men.*" The precise date of this circumstance is not given, but from other statements in his Journal, it appears to have occurred about 1753. It is not known in what barn Grimshaw preached.

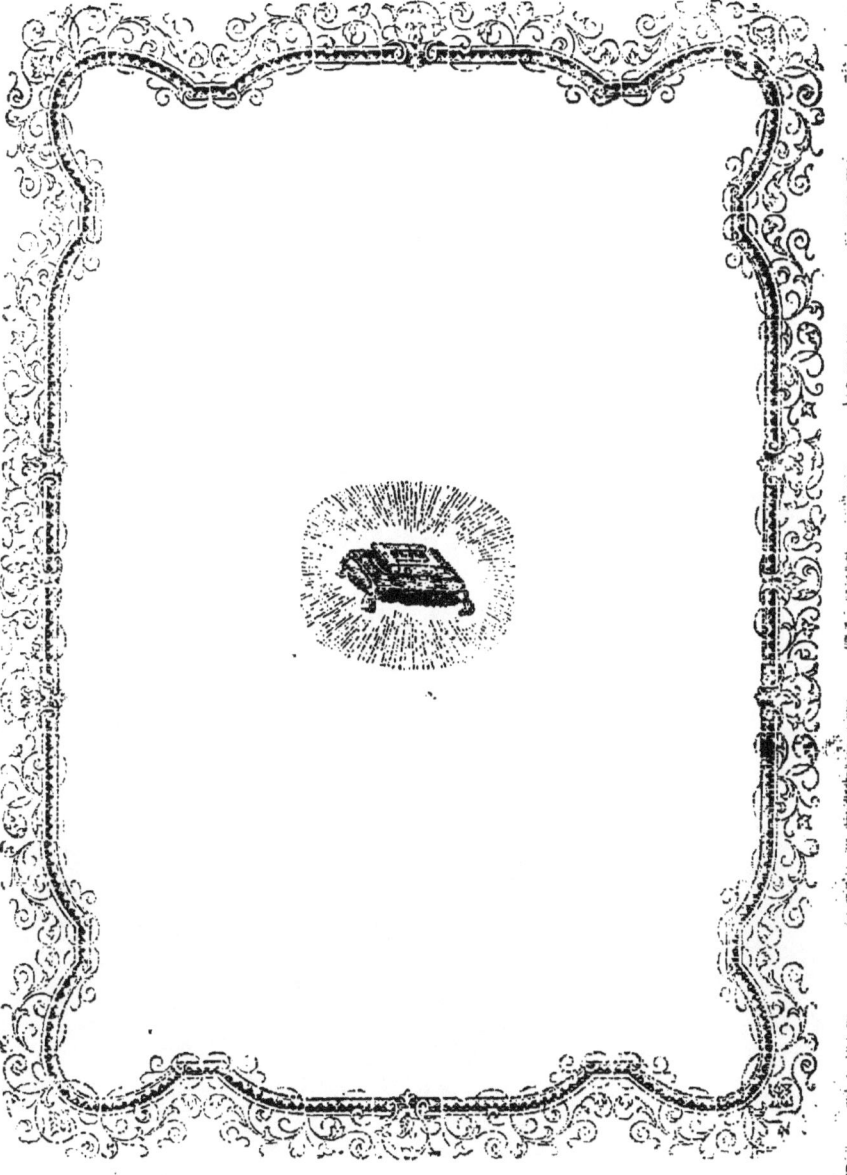

www.ingramcontent.com/pod-product-compliance
Lightning Source LLC
Chambersburg PA
CBHW031348160426
43196CB00007B/777